CULTURE SMART!
BRAZIL

Sandra Branco

with Rob Williams

·K·U·P·E·R·A·R·D·

ISBN 978 1 85733 689 4
This book is also available as an e-book: eISBN 978 1 85733 690 0

British Library Cataloguing in Publication Data
A CIP catalogue entry for this book is available from the British Library

First published in Great Britain
by Kuperard, an imprint of Bravo Ltd
59 Hutton Grove, London N12 8DS
Tel: +44 (0) 20 8446 2440 Fax: +44 (0) 20 8446 2441
www.culturesmart.co.uk
Inquiries: sales@kuperard.co.uk

Distributed in the United States and Canada
by Random House Distribution Services
1745 Broadway, New York, NY 10019
Tel: +1 (212) 572-2844 Fax: +1 (212) 572-4961
Inquiries: csorders@randomhouse.com

Series Editor Geoffrey Chesler
Design Bobby Birchall

Printed in Malaysia

Cover image: *The famous steps in Rio de Janeiro covered in fragments of tiles, ceramics, and mirrors by the artist Jorge Selarón.* © iStock

The photographs on pages 97, 114, 115 (bottom), 118, 126, 133, 136, 140, and 162 are reproduced by permission of the authors.

Images on the following pages reproduced under Creative Commons Attribution-Share Alike 3.0 Unported license: 13 © Gfonsecabr; 16 © http://veton.picq.fr; 17 © en:User:Cburnett; 19 © Malene Thyssen; 21 © Bgabel; 24 © Artyominc; 27 © Martin St-Amant (S23678); 28 © Brasu; 58 © No author info.; 71 © Alvesgaspar; 73 (top) © Isha; 74 © FrankOWeaver; 75 © Junius; 84 © Diogo Dubiella; 113 © Claitonmedina; 115 (top) Felix Tansil; 116 © nwerneck; 121 © Henrique Dante de Almeida; 125 (top) © Felipe.acan; 135 © Luan Lenon. Reproduced under Creative Commons Attribution 3.0 Brazil license: 48 © Ricardo Stuckert (Presidency of the Republic); 79 © Tânia Rêgo/ABr; 86 (left) © Foto:Antônio Cruz/ABr; 91 © Valter Campanato/ABr. Under Creative Commons Attribution-Share Alike 2.5 Generic license: 94 © Osmar Arouck; 120 (top) © Leonardo "Leguas" Carvalho. Under Creative Commons Attribution-Share Alike 2.0 Generic license: 15 © Emerson Santana Pardo; 18 © Ricardo Polisel Alves; 20 © tiago araujo from Minas Gerais, Brasil; 22 © Lea Maimone; 50 © Gianluca Ramalho Misiti; 55 © Thiago Melo; 85 © Sergio Luiz; 86 (right) © Prefeitura de Olinda; 109 © Elizabetsyatbu; 125 (bottom) © Fernando Dall'Acqua; 129 © Rodrigo Soldon. Pages 98, 104, 107, 123 © Shutterstock

About the Authors

SANDRA BRANCO is a Brazilian-born writer now living in the UK. After graduating in Communications from São Paulo University she worked as a video and television producer and scriptwriter in São Paulo, Rio de Janeiro, Recife, Bahia, and Ceará, before going on to gain an MA in Screenwriting at the Northern School of Film and Television in Leeds. She now lives and works in London.

ROB WILLIAMS is a principal lecturer in the Department of Modern Languages and Cultures at the University of Westminster in London, where he runs an MA program in International Liaison and Communication. He has lived and worked in France, Spain, Germany, the United States, China, and Brazil. He is also a consultant in intercultural communication.

The Culture Smart! series is continuing to expand.
For further information and latest titles visit
www.culturesmart.co.uk

The publishers would like to thank **CultureSmart!**Consulting for its help in researching and developing the concept for this series.

CultureSmart!Consulting creates tailor-made seminars and consultancy programs to meet a wide range of corporate, public-sector, and individual needs. Whether delivering courses on multicultural team building in the USA, preparing Chinese engineers for a posting in Europe, training call-center staff in India, or raising the awareness of police forces to the needs of diverse ethnic communities, it provides essential, practical, and powerful skills worldwide to an increasingly international workforce.

For details, visit www.culturesmartconsulting.com

CultureSmart!Consulting and **CultureSmart!** guides have both contributed to and featured regularly in the weekly travel program "Fast Track" on BBC World TV.

contents

contents

Map of Brazil

introduction

For many people Brazil conjures up images of football, *Carnaval*, and the finest coffee in the world. But the country is much more than beaches and bossa nova, although the sound of samba is an excellent starting point for exploring this vibrant, captivating, and infinitely complex land.

Brazil is at once stunningly beautiful and delightfully disorganized. Even though it is one of the ten largest economies in the world, poverty exists side by side with spectacular wealth. As part of the New World, it is open to new ideas, new technologies, and newcomers. Youthful and fast moving, it can overwhelm you with its sheer size, or the warmth and spontaneity of its people, while its street children and shantytowns can be quite unsettling.

The fundamental concept to understand is that there is not one but several Brazils, not only because of its varied geography and racial mix, but also in time: sixteenth-century ways coexist with twenty-first century lifestyles. Brazil is home to the so-called "lung of the world," the Amazon forest, and its incredible biodiversity. It also comes with its fair share of regional differences. It is a true melting pot of races and cultures—the Brazilians are a colorful mixture of native indigenous people, black former slaves, white

Europeans, and Asian and Middle Eastern immigrants. Despite this, there is a strong sense of national identity.

Brazil is the biggest country in South America and the fifth largest in the world. It builds satellites, exports airplanes, has its own petroleum industry, and takes pride in its modern architecture, furniture, fashion, and picturesque colonial towns. It has four different time zones, a rain forest, an Atlantic forest, drylands, wetlands, flatlands, high mountains, skyscrapers, busy urban centers, and quite a few deserted beaches hidden away in the 4,655 miles (7,491 km) of coastline.

One cannot hope to do justice to such diversity in a single book, and some generalization is inevitable. *Culture Smart! Brazil* aims to help you discover this fascinating country for yourself. It introduces the Brazilian people, their values, customs, and traditions; how they go about their daily life and spend their leisure time; and the way they think and do business. It describes the historical circumstances and influences that have shaped Brazilian society. The focus is mainly, though not exclusively, on the middle class—since these are the people visitors are most likely to interact with—so you will be eased into your first encounters with the Brazilians and their culture.

Key Facts

Official Name	Republica Federativa do Brasil (Federal Republic of Brazil)	
Capital City	Brasília	Population 2,562,963 (2013)
Major Cities (by Population)	São Paulo, Rio de Janeiro, Belo Horizonte, Porto Alegre, Brasília, Recife, Salvador, Curitiba	
Area	3,286,470 sq. miles (8,511,965 sq. km)	
Climate	Tropical and subtropical	
Currency	Real	
Population	201,032,714 (2013)	
Ethnic Makeup	White 47.7%; Mixed Race 43.1%; Black 7.6%; Oriental 1.1%; Indigenous 0.4% (2010 census)	
Language	Portuguese	
Main Religions	No official religion. Predominantly Roman Catholic. Growing Evangelical movement	Other religions include: Mormons, Eastern Orthodox, Judaism, Islam, Buddhism, and Spiritualism (Kardecism, African, and Native Indian).
Government	Federal Republic, governed by Executive, Legislature, and Judiciary at national and state levels	Bicameral legislature: the Chamber of Deputies and the Senate. Presidential elections are held every four years.

Media	The main network TV channels are Globo, SBT, Record, and Bandeirantes. Main paid TV providers are NET, SKY, Claro TV, VIVO TV, Oi TV, and GVT TV. There are over 9,000 radio stations.	The newspapers with the widest circulation are *Folha de São Paulo, Jornal do Brasil, O Globo*, and *O Estado de São Paulo*.
Media: English Language	*Folha de São Paulo:* www1.folha.uol.com.br/internacional/en *Valor Econômico* (business newspaper): www.valor.com.br/international	
Electricity	220 volts and/or 110–127 volts	Several electricity grids supply electricity at different voltages.
TV/Video	PAL M and NTSC	DVD Region 4
Internet Domain	.br	
Telephone	Country code: 55	The code for dialing out depends on the phone company you use.
Time Zones	There are four time zones: Standard Brasília Time, GMT minus 3 hours (majority of the country); Western Area, GMT minus 4 hours; Acre, GMT minus 5 hours; Fernando de Noronha, GMT minus 2 hours.	Some parts of the country adopt summer time (generally from October to February).

LAND & PEOPLE

If you could choose only one word to describe Brazil, it would be diversity. The variety of landscape, climate, flora, fauna, racial types, and lifestyles is enormous.

Brazilians tend to think of their country as some sort of continent within South America. The reason may be that its land mass represents nearly half (47.3%) of the territory. Looking at the map, we can see that the entire east side of Brazil is coastline (Atlantic Ocean), while the west side borders almost all the other South American countries, except for Chile and Ecuador.

Since Brazil is mostly situated south of the equator, the seasons are the reverse of those in Europe and the USA. Officially, summer lasts from December 22 to March 21, fall from March 22 to June 21, winter from June 22 to September 21, and spring from September 22 to December 21. In parts of the country, however, notably the Amazon region, seasonal divisions are less clearly marked and tend to be classified as "wet" and "dry."

Brazil has four time zones. Brasília time is the nation's official standard, three hours behind Greenwich Mean Time (GMT), London.

The equator crosses the north of the country, near the city of Macapá. The Tropic of Capricorn passes through the south, near the city of São Paulo. This means that most of the country is within the tropical zone and characterized by a hot and humid climate. However, tropical does not necessarily mean that every region is hot all year-round, nor that the countryside is filled with lush vegetation. Altitude, proximity to the sea, soil fertility, and prevailing winds and weather fronts all have an effect on the different regions of the country.

The north is hotter and the south cooler (temperatures in some parts can fall below zero and snow is even seen occasionally in some cities). Generally speaking, cities on the coast are more humid, while those located on plateaus inland, such as Brasilia, São Paulo, and Belo Horizonte, have more temperate climates.

More specifically, Brazil can be divided into six climate zones: equatorial, tropical, Atlantic tropical, semiarid, highland tropical, and subtropical, according to location and terrain.

BRAZIL'S CLIMATE ZONES

In the Amazon region, which is equatorial, temperatures average 71–79°F (22–26°C), though at times it can be much hotter, and it rains often and heavily. Indeed, there are two areas where rainfall reaches over 78 inches (2,000 mm) a year: in the upper Amazon and near the city of Belém.

Most of central Brazil, parts of the northeast, and parts of the southeast have a tropical climate, characterized by hot, humid summers and colder, drier winters. Average temperature is around 68°F (20°C).

As its name suggests, the Atlantic tropical climate zone affects the coastline from Rio Grande do Norte down to the state of Paraná. Here rainfall is intense at different times of the year (fall and winter in the northeast and summer in the south). Temperatures can vary between 64 and 79°F (18 and 26°C), though as with other parts of the country they can rise to near 100°F (38°C) in summer.

The dryland inland part of the northeast, or sertão, is semiarid and suffers from long periods of drought. Temperatures average 80°F (27°C) but can soar above 100°F (38°C).

Along the plateau that stretches across the southeastern states of São Paulo, Minas Gerais, and parts of Paraná and Mato Grosso do Sul (highland tropical), temperatures average around 64–71°F (18–22°C). Rainfall can be very heavy during the summer. In the area along the border of the mountain range (Serra do Mar) in the state of São Paulo it rains almost as much as in the Amazon. However, winters are drier with occasional frost in some areas.

The area south of the Tropic of Capricorn has a subtropical climate. Here, despite hot summers, average temperatures are lower than 64°F (18°C) and can drop below freezing in winter.

THE REGIONS
Brazil is divided into five administrative regions. The characteristics of their inhabitants are highly influenced by their geographic and economic situations.

North
Amazonas – Pará – Acre – Rondônia – Roraima – Amapá – Tocantins

Also known as the Amazon region, the North region is mainly covered by rain forest and is sparsely populated. It rains often and so regularly that the locals tend to organize their day and even arrange meetings

and appointments for "before the rain" or "after the rain."

Despite recent deforestation, there are still large areas where, if you fly over the jungle, all you can see is an immense green carpet from horizon to horizon, with hardly a sign of human habitation.

Reservations have been set up for different tribes of Native Indians (*índios*) and most of the larger groups live in these areas. Most maintain contact with Brazilian institutions, and just a few do not welcome strangers. It is thought that there are still more groups that have yet to come into contact with outsiders.

The Amazon is the world's largest river in volume and its annual outflow accounts for one-fifth of the world's fresh water entering the sea. It is not surprising, then, that much of the transport in the region is by boat.

Given the difficulty in policing such a vast area, some illegal settlers, traders, and even drug traffickers have taken advantage and there have sometimes been violent clashes with the indigenous groups. Nowadays there is an integrated mapping system linked to satellite photography (*imazongeo*) to monitor the whole area and identify illegal use of land.

The harvesting of Brazil nuts and rubber latex are still the main economic activities, together with manufacturing, mining, and logging. Industry, farming, and ecotourism play only a small role.

Originally agriculture and mining were encouraged, although this resulted in jungle-sized environmental problems and the deforestation of about 14 percent of the rain forest (an area about the size of France). The government has since launched a series of policies to control development, such as the prohibition of timber export. This has managed to halve the pace of deforestation, and the vast majority of the rain forest is still preserved undamaged.

The Amazon forest contains the largest single reserve of biological organisms in the world. Even though nobody knows how many different species inhabit it, scientists estimate that they represent  15–30 percent of all species on the planet.

The region has powerful folklore traditions, mainly with indigenous origins, that are kept alive by the *caboclos*—mixed descendants of Portuguese and Native Indians.

The two main cities in the North are Manaus and Belém do Pará.

The state of Acre and the western corner of the state of Amazonas are five hours behind GMT and two hours behind Brasília Time, while the rest of Amazonas, and the states of Rondônia, Roraima, and the western half of the state of Pará are four hours behind GMT or one hour behind Brasília Time. The eastern half of Pará and the state of Tocantins are three hours behind GMT at standard Brasília Time.

Northeast
Maranhão – Piauí – Ceará – Rio Grande do Norte – Paraíba – Pernambuco – Bahia – Alagoas – Sergipe – Fernando de Noronha (island territory)

Perhaps the biggest contrasts within any region can be found in the Northeast. Nearly 30 percent of Brazilians live here, and the difference between rich and poor is very marked.

The coast is beautiful, with palm beaches and warm waters that attract considerable domestic and foreign tourism. The number of visitors to the island of Fernando de Noronha is severely restricted because of its status as an ecological sanctuary where research and conservation projects are

carried out all year. The land on the coastal plain is very fertile and devoted mainly to sugar plantations.

In the interior, however, lie the drylands, or *sertão*. This area suffers regular and lengthy droughts, resulting in large-scale misery and migration. The people of this area (*sertanejos*) leave their homes either to work in the sugar plantations during the drought period, or for good, heading to big urban centers within the Northeast or in the Southeast, where they often end up unemployed and homeless.

The transitional zone between the coastal plain and the *sertão* is called the *agreste* and is devoted to cattle rearing. In the cities the service sector plays an important economic role. Since the recent discovery of sizeable oil fields off the coastline, the region has begun to develop economically and is attracting greater domestic and international investment.

Pernambuco and Bahia, where most of the oil fields have been found, were the main colonial centers and their resonance in Brazilian culture is strong. They have the richest folklore and inspire

most of the music, cuisine, and the so-called
"typically Brazilian" culture.

The region was also home to resistance centers
(*quilombos*), created and controlled by black
runaway slaves who organized themselves in self-
sufficient communities. The most successful of
these were in Pernambuco. Nowadays, Salvador,
capital of Bahia, is the center for black consciousness
and culture in Brazil.

People who live on the coast tend to be more
laid-back and easygoing than those from inland.
They say the *sertanejos* are as tough as the land
they live on. Because of the heat, whenever possible,
northeastern people have longer lunch hours or
even take a half-hour nap after lunch. However,
services and shops do not tend to close for lunch
and work normal commercial hours.

The largest cities in the Northeast are Salvador,
Fortaleza, and Recife.

The entire Northeast region is three hours
behind GMT at standard Brasília Time, except for

Fernando de Noronha, which is two hours behind GMT and one hour ahead of standard Brasília Time.

Central West
Mato Grosso – Mato Grosso do Sul – Goiás – Federal District of Brasília

This region covers most of the country's central plateau (*planalto central*). An area of widespread savannas and tropical grasslands, it is still sparsely populated.

In order to encourage migration and development in the remote and isolated Central West region, President Kubitschek (1955–60) moved Brazil's capital from Rio de Janeiro to "the middle of nowhere," as some called it then. The result was the planned city of Brasília, the "capital of hope." For many years, however, Brasília remained a dormitory city for politicians. It can still feel a little bit like an overgrown university campus, where you need to drive or take the bus to go across town and

where sidewalks do not exist on the main roads.
The place is nonetheless lightened by the stunning
curves of buildings by architect Oscar Niemeyer.

The region is also home to one of Brazil's most
famous ecotourist destinations, the Pantanal
swamplands in Mato Grosso. People come to
explore diverse fauna and flora, see multitudes
of colorful birds, and spot caimans.

Due to a rapid expansion in industrial farming,
the savanna ecosystem has suffered a great deal,
being reduced to only 20 percent of its original size.
Agro-industry and cattle-raising remain the major
economic activities.

The federal government has kept back large
areas in the region as reservations for the
indigenous tribes who first lived there. Although
the overwhelming majority of Brazilians express
very protective views about native groups and
their right to the land, those who live near the
reservations have more mixed opinions. Some
people seem to resent the fact that the tribes are

given a lot of land while they have to work hard to buy a small plot.

In spite of the best efforts of the State and a slow increase in migration to the area, some parts of this region still remain remote, allowing for highly exploitative work practices to take place.

The main cities in the Central West are Brasília, Goiânia, Campo Grande, and Cuiabá.

Mato Grosso and Mato Grosso do Sul are four hours behind GMT and one hour behind Brasília Time. The Federal District of Brasília and the state of Goiás are three hours behind GMT at standard Brasília Time.

Southeast
Minas Gerais – Espírito Santo – Rio de Janeiro – São Paulo

Most of Brazil's population is concentrated in this region. It has been called "the heart of Brazil" (or sometimes its "brain") because of the major economic role it plays. It has the best-developed industry together with the most advanced agriculture, and São Paulo as both the main financial and commercial center of the country.

The region is rich in minerals and gems; it produces coffee and grains for export, plus a variety of foodstuffs, dairy, and meat products for the domestic market. It is also the traditional manufacturing base of the country. Tourism plays a significant part, particularly in the city of Rio de Janeiro and the historic towns of Minas Gerais. Minas contains a series of well-kept picturesque colonial towns with some of the best examples of Brazilian baroque art, which is unique and less ornate than the European version.

The coastline is stunningly framed by the mountains of the Serra do Mar, with some preserved areas of Atlantic forest. Mountain formations are everywhere and characterize some of the famous pictures of Brazil, such as the Pão de Açúcar (Sugar Loaf Mountain) in Rio.

São Paulo state is a land of immigrants, with descendants from all groups who declare themselves proud of being Brazilians and *paulistas* (inhabitants of São Paulo state). Its capital, also called São Paulo, is the largest metropolitan area in the country and ranks fifth in the world, with a population of over twenty million. It is the main Brazilian destination for foreign business travelers. *Paulistanos*, the inhabitants of São Paulo city, are individualistic, dynamic, and workaholic. Most people work long hours and many have more than one job. It is truly a cosmopolitan center and its cuisine and art reflect this in their international flavor. There are more Italians (and Italian descendants) in São Paulo than in Rome. Modern travelers from Japan find in the district of Liberdade a community that keeps prewar Japanese customs and traditions. Personal safety is also a concern, and 70 percent of Brazil's bullet proofed automobiles (two-hundred a day) are sold there. The wealthy have taken to using helicopters to get around (partly also to avoid the huge traffic jams). São Paulo now has the most helicopters in the world – more than New York or Tokyo.

Rio de Janeiro, host city for the 2016 Olympic Games, remains the Brazilian picture postcard for foreigners and the main tourist destination, especially during *Carnaval*. Its laid-back charm and beach lifestyle even inspired the Disney studios in the 1940s, when they created a character called "Zé Carioca," who loves samba. Rio is the second-biggest Brazilian city, with a population of over six million. It is home to the mega studios of TV Globo, the most influential national network and one of the largest in the world (see Chapter 9, under The Media). *Cariocas* (inhabitants of Rio) claim theirs is "the most beautiful city," and contest São Paulo's claim to be "the most important city."

There is a permanent rivalry between Rio and São Paulo. Although sometimes disguised, it can be found in the most unsuspected places. Therefore, any visitor socializing or doing business in either city should be cautious before expressing any opinion about one or the other. Despite their claims, both Rio de Janeiro and São Paulo share the harsh realities of high-level noise, pollution, traffic, violence, and crime.

Mineiros, people from Minas Gerais, are thought of as serious and hardworking. They can be more private and reserved on initial contact, although they are very hospitable.

The state capitals in the Southeast are Belo Horizonte, Vitória, Rio de Janeiro, and São Paulo.

The entire Southeast region is three hours behind GMT at standard Brasília Time.

South
Paraná – Santa Catarina – Rio Grande do Sul

With a cooler climate, the South is supposed to be the region with the best quality of life. It is a highly developed area, its major economic activities being cattle raising, agro-industry, the production of grains and a growing wine industry, though it keeps a balance between the rural and manufacturing sectors. It is home to Itaipu, one of the largest hydroelectric dams in the world.

The coast of Santa Catarina, in particular the city of Florianópolis, is a summer tourist destination for domestic visitors as well as a considerable number of Argentinians. On the border between Brazil and Argentina, the Iguaçu Falls is one of Brazil's most magnificent sights and the region's main tourist attraction for domestic and international visitors. A recent trend has placed it on the international list of wedding destinations, catching the fancy of brides and grooms in search of an exotic location.

The southern highlands were once covered by subtropical forests with a predominance of araucária pine trees. Expanding agro-industry, however, resulted in it being heavily deforested and just a few pockets of pine forest remain.

Further south, the region shares the wide plains or *pampas* (homeland to *gaúchos*, the South American cowboys) with Uruguay and Argentina. They once hunted wild cattle and drank *chimarrão*, a strong tea made of the herb *mate*, prepared and served in a bowl with a silver straw. Drinking *chimarrão* is still one of the best-kept traditions in this region. The term *gaúcho* was originally used to describe the mixed descendants of Portuguese, Spanish, and indigenous (Guarani) populations. Nowadays it refers to all Rio Grande do Sul inhabitants.

The region cherishes its European heritage, being substantially composed of German, Italian, Slav, and Polish immigrant descendants. Blumenau, in Santa Catarina, is the center for German culture, following

the Germanic festive calendar, and keeping its traditions and cuisine, with an architecture to match. In Rio Grande do Sul, the Italian immigrants cultivated the first Brazilian vineyards. But it is the capital city of Curitiba that has attracted larger internal migration during recent years, after being given the title of Brazilian model city and because of its comfortable lifestyle.

The main cities in the South are Curitiba, Porto Alegre, Florianópolis, and Blumenau.

The entire South is three hours behind GMT at standard Brasília Time.

POPULATION

Brazil's population is now estimated at over 200 million, making it the fifth most populous country in the world. However, much of the country is sparsely populated and the overall population density is low. Most people congregate in the cities on the coast and in the Southeast, which is the center for industrial activity. Over 50 percent of Brazil's people are in the state of São Paulo alone.

Brazil is a young country—more than half the population are under twenty-nine years of age, although life expectancy is increasing. The population is still growing, albeit slowly, dropping from nearly 3 percent in the mid-twentieth century to about 1.2 percent in 2010. Added to that Brazil has one of the lowest fertility rates in Latin America, reported as 1.9 children per woman in 2010, lower than estimates for the USA, and similar to rates in Europe.

The turning point, both for the decline in growth and the increase in population movement within the country, seems to have been the 1970s. Economic modernization was a key factor. As cities developed, people left the land in search of work, and since the Southeast was the center for industrial production, many moved there from the Northeast in one of the largest internal migrations in recent history. This is still going on—São Paulo state received around a million migrants from the Northeast alone in the last decade—though the rate of migration has slowed. Attention is now turning to the less populated states of the North and Central West. Amapá saw a 100 percent increase in population over the last ten years.

Brazil is a truly multiethnic society, with just under half the country considering themselves white, just over 40 percent mixed race, and about 8 percent black. The remainder are divided between oriental and indigenous racial groups. There are now about 520,000 Native Indians living in territories set aside for them by the government. Many tribes maintain a lifestyle similar to the one they lived before the Europeans arrived. The indigenous territories cover 10 percent of the total area of Brazil, which is roughly equivalent to three times the size of Britain.

When you compare racial background and distribution of wealth, the image is not a positive one. The poorer Brazilians are, the darker their skins. Historically, when slavery was abolished, black labor was replaced by immigrant labor, with black communities struggling to find their place in society. A lot has changed since then, but probably not enough. Nowadays there are a few examples of very wealthy black people in the business world who did not make their money playing football (soccer). But the majority of Afro-Brazilians are found in the less privileged classes. In order to address the situation, a system of quotas has been adopted, guaranteeing them, for example, a percentage of places in the universities, similar to the system in the USA. The scheme has been very successful, although implementing it has not been simple. In a highly mixed society, deciding who is black is not a straightforward matter.

What is a Brazilian?

Brazilians are mainly descended from Native Indians, black African slaves, or white European settlers. They can also be *mulatos* (mixed white European and black African), *caboclos* (mixed white European and Native Indian), or *mamelucos* (mixed black African and Native Indian).

Apart from Portuguese, Spanish, and Dutch arrivals during colonial times, and later Italian, German, and Polish immigration, other large groups include immigrants from the Middle East, particularly Syria and Lebanon, and Japan.

More recently arrived communities include Koreans and South American nationals from neighboring countries.

As a rule, the Brazilian "love for the mixture" seems to be contagious and most groups end up contributing to the birth of new generations of colorful nationals. There is a nationwide feeling that every newcomer will enrich the original culture with their new set of practices and beliefs. One Brazilian pastime (and a way to start a conversation) is to ask someone for their surname, trying to guess their origins. Although Brazilians might come in all shapes, colors, and sizes, acceptance of difference is one thing that defines their identity.

Just How Mixed Are Brazilians?

"The Mormons in the United States had this rule that if you were black, you couldn't be a bishop in the church. When they came to Brazil, they couldn't decide who was black and so they changed the rule."

British historian Peter Burke in an interview with the *Folha de São Paulo* newspaper, November 2004

A BRIEF HISTORY
From the Jungle

Evidence of Paleo-Indians in the territory that later became Brazil goes back at least ten thousand years. By analyzing remains such as ceramic and cave art, archaeologists have found that some indigenous groups achieved a high level of cultural development.

There were a multitude of tribes scattered throughout the land with different customs and over

170 languages. Along the coast, the largest ones, or those that survived colonization, were the Tupis and the Guaranis, and most of the information about indigenous habits and beliefs refers to the Tupi-Guarani group.

Before the Europeans arrived, the Native Indians lived mainly in seminomadic tribal communities. The extended family shared the same habitation (*oca*), which was effectively a large communal hut where each member had the use of a hammock. Cooking was done outside by the women, who took turns in doing the domestic work, including taking care of all children from the community, not only their own. The men were responsible for tasks such as hunting and fishing, besides protecting their tribe. Each tribe had a chief (*cacique*) and a witch doctor (*pajé*), both male. The *pajé* was also in charge of the religious ceremonies, which were mostly for the men only. They were polytheists and their gods were mainly connected to nature, and arranged in a hierarchy, with the principal deity being Tupã, the Thunder God. Each tribe was autonomous, with no superior governing power.

Discovery
In spite of indications of a previous European presence, Brazil was officially discovered by the Portuguese navigator Pedro Álvares Cabral in April 1500. Cabral was apparently on an expedition to find the western route to India when a storm blew him off course, forcing him to land in a quiet bay in today's state of Bahia.

First reports equated the lush vegetation and the innocence of the new land's naked inhabitants with visions of an earthly paradise. This comparison did not survive closer inspection, with evidence of cannibalism among some of the tribes. Failing to identify easy riches such as gold and precious stones, the colonizers settled for exploiting a lucrative red dyewood known as *pau-brasil* ("brazilwood"), which later gave its name to the

country. Portuguese and French traders soon started shipping the timber to Europe.

Agriculture was the next step forward, but that was easier said than done since it meant living side by side with the natives. There was no central power to overthrow, and the settlers could not survive without the natives' knowledge of the forest. The only way to occupy the land was by reaching an agreement with the indigenous groups that allowed the colonizers to share part of that knowledge. Such a pact could certainly not be achieved by force. The settlers stumbled across the solution in the strangest of circumstances.

According to the indigenous tradition the only way to accept a stranger into a tribe was by blood ties, as the first Europeans to marry native women according to local custom found out. These were adventurous individuals who came looking for quick wealth and ended up staying, living with the tribes and taking advantage of the power that came with being both Indian and European.

The natives had no concept of sin, but the Catholic Portuguese did. Although the first men to accept indigenous values and live in accordance with them were fundamental to the colonization project, they were despised by their Christian colleagues. Once more, native customs came to the rescue. The traditional way of forming an alliance with a neighboring tribe was by offering a woman in marriage to its chief. The woman would then accept the customs of her husband's tribe instead of her own. With the proliferation of European communities and the arrival of Catholic priests, this arrangement enabled the new marriages to be accepted by both cultures. The new bride was declared "white" in the Portuguese community and the groom was considered "Indian" in his wife's tribe. This phenomenon formed the basis of a positive attitude with regard to racial mixing. But the Portuguese government used it as a form of control. It issued "purity of blood" certificates in exchange for "good behavior" and obedience from the new generations of mixed race Brazilians, and this underlined the importance of being "white."

Colonial Government
São Vicente, in today's coastal state of São Paulo, was the first Portuguese-organized settlement, founded in 1532. Salvador was established in 1549 by Brazil's first royal governor. More needed to be done, however, in order to encourage commercial exploration and development. The Portuguese

government divided the colony into fifteen areas of land (some bigger than Portugal) and made them "hereditary captaincies." These were given as a present from the king, and their owners (*donatários*) were supposed to maintain, defend, and exploit their land. This created a system of large estates that would influence the country throughout its history until modern times.

The captaincy of Pernambuco was very profitable as a result of highly productive sugar plantations. In order to work the land, the colonizers tried to enslave the Native Indians, but their work rate and productivity were low. Also, they had no immunity to Western diseases and many died. The solution was to import slave labor from West Africa. The sugar they produced was then exported to an eager European market.

No More Boundaries

Portugal and Spain had an agreement (the Treaty of Tordesillas, 1494) that divided any land discovered in the western hemisphere between the two countries. This line crossed the middle of modern Brazilian territory. With the death of the Portuguese King Dom Sebastião in 1578, his cousin the Spanish king united both nations under the Spanish crown. As there were no boundaries, the Brazilians went on inland expeditions searching for Eldorado and capitalized on anything they found, such as precious stones and Indian slaves. When Portugal recovered its independence from Spain in 1640, they kept the occupied lands. The Portuguese also succeeded in recovering the city of Olinda (Pernambuco) from a twenty-four-year Dutch occupation.

The First Synagogue of the Americas

When the Portuguese overthrew the Dutch, they also banished the Jews who had settled in Pernambuco. They were well established and in 1634 had already founded the first synagogue of the Americas in today's city of Recife. Once expelled, twenty-three of the Jews went to New Amsterdam (now New York) and founded the first Jewish community in what would become the USA.

The Golden Years

With the decline of Brazil's sugar economy, more inland expeditions were organized to search for gold and precious stones. Gold and diamonds were found in today's state of Minas Gerais (which means "general mines"). As a result, in 1763 the capital was moved south from Salvador to Rio de Janeiro, which was closer and a more direct link to Minas. The gold rush attracted both people from the northeastern coastal plantations and newcomers from Portugal. Much of Brazil's gold ended up in Britain through the purchase of textile products by the Portuguese and, according to some, helped pay for the British Industrial Revolution.

Just when the mining boom was weakening, an even greater source of riches materialized in the shape of coffee plantations further south.

The Kingdom of Portugal, the Algarve, and Brazil

In 1808, the Portuguese monarch and his court transferred from Lisbon to Rio de Janeiro to escape Napoleon's invasion of Portugal. This cunning plan resulted in Brazil being promoted in 1815 from colony to kingdom (as part of the Kingdom of Portugal, the Algarve, and Brazil) and, paradoxically, created favorable circumstances for Brazil's future independence.

Independence Days

Although Napoleon's reign ended in 1815, the Portuguese King João VI chose to stay in Brazil until 1821, when a political crisis threatened his power back home. He returned to Lisbon but left behind his son, Pedro, with the title of Viceroy Regent. Barely a year after his father's departure, the prince proclaimed Brazil's independence and had himself crowned Emperor Pedro I, even though he remained heir to the Portuguese throne. In order to be recognized as independent by Portugal, the new Brazilian government agreed to take over the very large debt the Portuguese owed Britain.

Emperor Dom Pedro abdicated the throne of Brazil in 1831, in favor of his son, Dom Pedro II, and returned to Lisbon to become King Pedro IV of Portugal.

Brazilian Monarchy

Dom Pedro II ruled for more than half a century. He was a competent administrator who advanced Brazil's political development and unity. His stable reign saw improvements to the infrastructure, the building of railroads, encouragement of immigration from Europe, and the consideration of health and welfare schemes for the whole country. Another change to the economy was the increase in coffee production, overtaking sugar as the national crop

and accounting for well over half of the country's total exports.

Support for the monarchy came mainly from the wealthy owners of coffee plantations, which depended on slave labor. The abolition of slavery in 1888, in response to British pressure, set off a reaction among the Emperor's supporters, generating a

series of parliamentary crises. In November 1889, Dom Pedro was deposed by the military, to the surprise of the general public. The transition to a republic happened without bloodshed as the royal family left the country for exile in France.

A Land of Immigrants

Leaving aside the European colonizers, the first wave of immigration, although not voluntary, occurred when millions of Africans were imported to work as slaves in the Brazilian plantations (from 1534 to 1888). The second wave was in 1808, when the country opened its ports to "friendly nations." Both emperors promoted European immigration, mainly to Brazil's south. Germans and Italians were offered plots of land and settled initially in today's states of Santa Catarina and Rio Grande do Sul.

The most significant influx, however, took place with the abolition of slavery. A change of policy meant that the new immigrants would no longer be small farmers but would come to work in the coffee plantations as laborers. Italians, Spaniards, and, later, Japanese, established themselves mostly in the state of São Paulo. This state also attracted Syrian and Lebanese tradesmen and merchants, although some settled in Rio de Janeiro and in the Amazon region, where they played a key role in the rubber trade between 1890 and 1910.

Café Latte Republic

The newborn republic established a federal arrangement that has continued to this day. A presidential system was adopted, replacing the old parliamentary one, and the former provinces were made into autonomous states.

This led to a power struggle between the central government and the new, independent states. The result was that the two most powerful states, São Paulo (whose economy was based on coffee) and Minas Gerais (whose wealth came from dairy farming), came to exercise a duopoly on power. They took turns nominating a candidate for the presidency, who was then duly elected. This became known as "coffee-with-milk politics."

The farming oligarchy that effectively controlled the country favored agricultural production and exports, and gave little incentive to the manufacturing sectors. But this "Old Republic" model was thrown into crisis as industry struggled to develop. The early 1920s brought expressions of discontent, with the first industrial strikes inspired by anarchist ideology (largely spread by Italian workers) and by the "lieutenants' movement" (*tenentismo*) inside the military. The lieutenants were mostly from poorer backgrounds and dissatisfied with the way the dominant oligarchy governed the country.

In Search of a Brazilian Identity

Revolutionary fervor and new ideas about national identity found form in a "Week of Modern Art" staged by Brazilian artists themselves in São Paulo in 1922. This was a rejection of the older, conservative, and essentially Europeanized Brazilian culture in favor of a new, fresh, and tropical model. The paintings were in bright, vibrant colors, while the literature featured racially mixed characters. This movement was also heavily influenced by the

industrial ideals of progress and development. It did more than revolutionize just the arts. The "Week" can be seen as symbolic of a society turning its back on the past and seeking to redefine itself; the impact of this event went far beyond the intellectual elite.

The New State

The balance of power between the presidents from São Paulo and Minas Gerais was upset when São Paulo's president failed to name a candidate from Minas to succeed him, appointing a *paulista* instead. Politicians from Minas joined forces with the prominent state of Rio Grande do Sul to name a southerner, former finance minister Getúlio Vargas, as their candidate, who had the support of the *tenentes* (lieutenants). Even though the candidate from São Paulo won the presidential elections in 1930, Vargas took power with the backing of the military. His first act was to dissolve the National Congress and the state and municipal legislatures. He replaced state governors with appointed officials. Drawing up a new constitution in 1934, he was elected for another term by indirect vote. In 1937, before the end of his new term and in response to civil unrest, he declared a state of emergency, citing a supposed threat of communism. Once again, he shut down the National Congress. But this time he revealed the dictatorial character of his regime by governing by decree, censoring the press, and arresting, torturing, and sending into exile opponents of the New State (*Estado Novo*), as he called it.

Vargas's policies were conducted in the name of nationalism. All the communication and transportation systems were nationalized. Domestic

industry was promoted and the importation of goods restricted. Vargas had a paternalist and populist image that appealed to a sector of the Brazilian people. He was seen as a strong figure who reduced the influence of the traditional oligarchies, partly by introducing secret ballots and women's voting rights. It also helped that his government passed very positive social welfare measures.

In 1945, as a result of military pressure, Vargas agreed to allow presidential elections and not to run himself. General Dutra, former minister of defense, won the elections and introduced more liberal economic policies along with reduced state intervention. In 1950, however, Vargas ran again and won the presidential election. His last term in office was colored by increasing protests about the stagnating economy and by accusations of corruption, so much so that the army, once his staunch supporter, demanded his resignation. Instead he put a bullet through his heart, causing the national commotion that, according to some, he had always sought.

Fifty Years in Five

The year 1955 saw a glimmer of democratic hope in the shape of the newly elected president, Juscelino Kubitschek. Entrepreneurial by nature, he promised to accomplish fifty years of progress in just five. In order to reverse years of economic decline, he encouraged both foreign and domestic investment and the rapid expansion of industry. His government oversaw increases in oil production and the establishment of a national petrochemical industry. Tax incentives for foreign companies helped the development of new industries, including automobile manufacturing.

Kubitschek was called a visionary and a madman, particularly when he announced and presided over the building of a new capital, Brasília. Completed in April 1960, the new capital was built from nothing in four years, in the remote Central West. The promised new era never came about, though. Instead, Brazilians had to cope with high inflation, caused mainly by the debt incurred by the huge road-building program that connected the major cities to each other and to the new capital.

The next president, Jânio Quadros, resigned a few months after winning the election. His vice president, a communist sympathizer, João Goulart, who succeeded him, did not finish his term. A military coup overthrew him in 1964. The darkest years in Brazil's modern history were to follow.

Dictatorship Years

Five generals held office during the period from 1964 to 1985. In the initial years they sought to stabilize the economic situation. In the name of an anticommunist campaign, "institutional acts" (decrees) closed down political parties, outlawed strikes, and allowed the persecution of all opponents of military rule. Student movements were severely repressed and student deaths at the hands of the police and the military provoked a reaction from different civil sectors, including the Catholic Church. More repression led to the beginning of armed resistance, organized mainly by students.

The military shut down the National Congress and issued new institutional acts censoring the media and passing laws that contravened human rights. Political opposition was met with torture and exile. Progressive sectors of the Catholic Church played a fundamental role in opposing the dictatorship. Despite being censored at home, Brazilian Bishop Hélder Câmara was the first to denounce the use of torture publically to the outside world, during one of his trips to France.

On the financial front, however, inflation was contained and the economy grew at one of the highest rates in the world (there was a 14 percent increase in GDP in 1973), attracting foreign investors. But successive petroleum crises quickly changed the economic landscape, since imported oil was the country's main energy source. The economy spiraled out of control and inflation shot up. As a result, people became increasingly dissatisfied with the government.

Liberation Theology

The more progressive sectors within the Catholic Church were organized around the ideals of Liberation Theology, which were most widespread in the 1970s and 1980s. This supported a social vision of the Christian promise of salvation and prayed for better economic, social, and political conditions for all people on earth (not just in heaven). Its proponents established ecclesiastical communities (*comunidades eclesiais de base*), which acted as centers of discussion and influenced a whole generation of Catholics, including former President Lula da Silva.

A steady reinstatement of civil liberties began in 1974, with the suspension of press censorship. In 1979, there was a general amnesty for political exiles and the military alike. In 1982 the first direct elections for state governors, suspended since 1965, took place.

Despite popular pressure for direct presidential elections, in 1984 the candidate of the opposition coalition, Tancredo Neves, was chosen by an electoral college. The first civilian president after twenty-one years of military government did not rule the country; he died weeks after taking office, and was replaced by his vice president. The dictatorship was nevertheless ended, as was the longest transition to democracy in Latin America.

Impeachment or Resignation

The first direct elections for president since 1960 took place in November 1989. Fernando Collor won a narrow victory over the socialist Workers' Party candidate, Lula da Silva. Collor struggled to control the hyperinflation that had overtaken his predecessor's government, but he failed to stabilize the economy and avoid recession and was himself charged with corruption. When the trial for his impeachment started, Collor resigned. However, the Senate, by a large majority, reached a verdict to impeach him.

Once again, a Brazilian vice president took office. Itamar Franco governed for the remaining two years of the term. His priority was to design an economic plan to control inflation, and this was made the responsibility of finance minister Fernando Henrique Cardoso.

The Real Plan

Fernando Henrique Cardoso, a former social scientist, was elected—and reelected—over Lula da Silva, mainly because of the success of his program to contain inflation. He changed the name of the currency to the Real, and adopted a plan of austerity measures, which became known as the "Real Plan" (Plano Real). The average rate of inflation dropped from 1,280.9 percent per annum (as during the previous five years) to an average of 11.4 percent per annum by the year 2000. His other priorities included the improvement of the national health system and the expansion of elementary education, resulting in a dramatic fall in illiteracy rates.

The Workers' Party

Former metalworker and trade unionist Luiz Inácio Lula da Silva won the presidency in 2002 with over 60 percent of votes. Lula was the first Brazilian from a disadvantaged background to reach the office of president. In a country with a tradition of controlling oligarchies and a military class that intervenes every now and then, electing a poor northeasterner as a president—and having him take office—was a remarkable achievement, regardless of the merits of his government. Those who believed that this was the end of control by a wealthy few over millions of poorer citizens would be deeply disappointed—as would those who expected the end of corruption in Brazilian politics.

One of the most significant steps taken by President Lula was that of ensuring the continuity of economic policy. This broke with the habits of previous governments, which often introduced radical economic shock tactics to solve the country's problems. For the first time in recent history there was no break in economic policy, sending signals to international investors of longer-term stability—and these were definitely picked up by the world markets.

It was, however, the "Bolsa Família" social benefit scheme that was mainly responsible for delivering Lula a second term. Introduced in 2003, Bolsa Família is a guaranteed minimum income scheme aimed at

families suffering from extreme and persistent poverty. Households receiving the benefit must commit to ensuring that children up to fifteen years old have an 85 percent record of school attendance, while youths aged sixteen to seventeen are required to complete 75 percent of school attendance. Every member of each household also has to attend regular health checks.

Lula's social plans managed to contribute to a significant reduction of poverty in Brazil, reaching around 13 million households, or 25 percent of the total, and thus addressing social exclusion.

Meanwhile, measures to deal with the issue of racial exclusion, which started with the adoption of racial quotas for students entering university during Fernando Henrique's government, were successfully implemented throughout Lula's government and became wider reaching during the term of Lula's successor, President Dilma Rousseff.

Elected in 2011, Dilma Rousseff is the first woman president—and the first economist—to take office in Brazil. In her youth, Dilma actively opposed the dictatorship and was jailed and tortured by the regime back then. She rose to power as Minister of Energy and Chief of Staff to President Lula, and in 2013 was ranked second in Forbes' list of the most powerful women in the world after Angela Merkel, Chancellor of Germany. Despite this, many believe that Lula continues to influence her government, acting as a co-president.

Dilma's government attracted the attention of the domestic and international media during the 2013 outcry, when more than a million people took to the streets of Brazil's cities, initially to protest at an increase in bus fares. Thanks to the power of the social media,

the protests quickly turned into a nationwide movement against bad public services, inflation, corruption, and other targets, also expressing outrage at the billions being spent on the World Cup. However, the protests had no real leadership. They were more the outpouring of disparate groups (or sometimes even individuals), each with their own claim.

There were violent clashes between some protesters and police. But in a country where since the dictatorship police training has focused on repression rather than peaceful crowd control, it is difficult to determine how the violence started.

Violence was also directed against the established media, mainly the TV news, which was accused of not listening to the streets. Nevertheless, overall the demonstrations were peaceful. They were not connected to any political party. On the contrary, several protestors chanted "No violence, no parties"

and did not tolerate party flags during the demonstrations.

Dilma's reaction to the street movement surprised some. She endorsed the right of citizens to take the streets peacefully, and sounded as if she opposed her own government. She also pledged to improve urban transport, health and education, and to make Brazil's political system more accountable.

The scale of the manifestation caught Brazilian politicians unprepared. Without a leader with whom to negotiate, they were not equipped to handle the situation, or indeed to know what to make of a "social media revolution" demanding transparency in politics and policies that were not necessarily linked to parties or ideologies.

The estimated 40 million individuals lifted out of poverty by the Bolsa Família policy has created a new class with access to education and the consumer market, adding their voices to the established middle classes in demanding better management of government money and adequate public services. But more than everything, this new generation of citizens seems to want to belong. They are claiming the streets—the public spaces—as a forum to discuss not only economic matters but also access to education, culture, the arts. They are questioning the political structures, the political system (there are talks of a new constitution), and they believe they can make a difference in shaping the country for the better. The road to becoming a developed country may be steeper than some of Brazil's more traditional politicians had in mind.

BRAZIL IN THE WORLD TODAY
Boom or Gloom?

The "B" in the "BRICS," Brazil has experienced an economic boom for over a decade and is seen as one of the most promising emerging markets. Foreign links and relations, forged under the presidency of Fernando Henrique, were strengthened and expanded by Lula. The discovery of oil fields fuelled the interest of foreign investors. At the same time Brazilian cosmetics, fashion, and design gained more than a foothold in cities in Europe and elsewhere in the developed world.

Brazil's Bolsa Família social program has inspired policy makers in Asia and Africa, and has led other Latin American countries in poverty reduction schemes. Such social policies have helped to establish a new middle class (and a new marketplace for global commerce) and this, together with a growth in Brazilian multinational companies, inspired greater international confidence. "Latin America's economic powerhouse" attracted record levels of foreign investment, as well as more immigrants from surrounding countries.

But then the realities of "*custo Brazil*," the operational costs associated with doing business in Brazil, hit home. Excessive bureaucracy, complicated and inefficient legislation, inefficient public services, high taxes, high interest rates, expensive labour costs, economic cartels, corruption within the public sector, and high transport costs due to poor infrastructure, are all challenges for foreign investors, and have been eroding Brazil's competitiveness. The increasing value of Brazil's currency has also hurt exports.

High business costs, together with financial crises in Europe and America and a slowdown in the Chinese economy, have resulted in a decline in foreign investment. After a celebrated growth of 7.5 percent in 2010, GDP was projected to grow by 3.2 percent in 2013 (according to Brazil's Central Bank).

Brazilian economists complain that the country's ability to negotiate trade deals is also hampered by the rules of Mercosul (the South-American trade block formed by Argentina, Brazil, Bolivia, Paraguay, Uruguay, and Venezuela), which prohibit member countries from unilaterally signing trade deals.

However, Brazil seems to be warming to the idea of altering the rules to allow each member to negotiate trade deals at their own pace and convenience. This tendency could be strengthened by the election of Brazilian diplomat Roberto Azevedo, an advocate of multilateralism, as the World Trade Organization's new director general. President Dilma applauded his appointment as a victory that gives developing nations a voice in a trade club that has long been dominated by the rich countries from the northern hemisphere. Brazil finally has a seat at the top table.

It is not just on the economic stage that Brazil has been exercising its new-found status. After taking part in thirty-three United Nations peacekeeping operations, acting as a mediator in the unrest in Venezuela in 2003, helping Colombia's government conduct rescue missions for hostages held by the FARC, and having continuously led a UN peacekeeping mission to Haiti since 2004, Brazil, a founding member of the UN, has been lobbying hard as a representative for South America and for the emerging economies. But its "Holy Grail"—a permanent seat on a newly expanded Security Council—is unlikely to be within reach soon. In spite of backing by the UK, France, Germany, and Japan, the inclusion of new permanent members implies a reform in the UN Security Council. This goes against the interest of some permanent members, who will do their best to delay it.

Even though the choice of Roberto Azevedo to head the WTO may be seen as a change in the world order, and as scoring a point for Brazil, there is no denying that the country is facing hard times—and it will have to come to terms with its political, economic, and logistical problems.

Brazilian optimists point to the country's size, natural resources, commodities, and its huge internal consumer market, as an opportunity too tempting to be ignored by international business.

Hosting the World Cup in 2014 and the Olympic Games in 2016 promises the possibility of a short-term boost to growth and prosperity. Of course, things could go terribly wrong if the costs of sports facilities and infrastructure turn into an economic burden for the future. But any improvement in Brazil's precarious infrastructure will be much welcomed.

GOVERNMENT

The present constitution of Brazil was drawn up in 1988 and new government mechanisms were put in place at that time. At the national level, power is administered by the executive, the legislature, and the judiciary. The same system is replicated at state level. As in the USA, the president is elected for a four-year term and appoints ministers of state. He or she may serve only two terms.

Brazil has thirty registered political parties, and there may be more to come before the next elections. The number of political parties means that it is almost impossible for any one party to govern on its own.

The government in 2014 was a coalition made up of eight left-wing parties: the Workers' Party (PT), Brazilian Socialist Party (PSB), Brazilian Communist Party (PCdoB), Democratic Workers' Party (PDT), Progressive Party (PP), Republican Party (PR), Brazilian Republican Party (PRB), and the Brazilian Democratic Movement (PMDB).

Two houses form the National Legislature: the Chamber of Deputies and the Federal Senate. States elect members to the Chamber of Deputies every four a with the number of deputies representing the state in proportion to its population. Three senators are elected from each state to the Senate and serve an eight-year term. In order for there to be continuity, the Senate elections are staggered: every four years one third, then two thirds, of seats are contested. At

the moment there are 81 senators and 513 deputies, who can run for reelection as many times as they (or their party) want.

The Federal Supreme Court, the highest court in the land, is composed of eleven judges. Below it are the Superior Court of Justice and the regional courts. Special courts deal with specific issues such as labor disputes and electoral or military matters.

There are twenty-three ministries, including finance, trade, domestic affairs, and foreign affairs. The Ministry for Planning, Budget, and Management, though, is separate from the Finance Ministry. There are two Ministries for Development (agrarian and social). Perhaps this shows a desire to enshrine checks and balances in money management, on the one hand, and an understanding of the need for social development, on the other. There is even a Ministry for National Integration.

In Brazil voting is considered a voluntary right from the ages of sixteen to eighteen and after sixty-four, and a compulsory duty between eighteen and sixty-four. Every citizen between these ages has to vote or give a good reason why they could not.

chapter two

VALUES & ATTITUDES

NATIONAL IDENTITY: SIZE MATTERS

When it comes to defining the makeup of the Brazilian people, there may be many regional differences and accents, but living in a big country is one thing that really matters. Until recently, most Brazilians did not travel abroad and economic migration was something that happened inside the country.

There is a feeling of self-sufficiency, not only because of Brazil's size and growing economic wealth, but also because of its language. Brazil is the only country in Latin America that speaks Portuguese and sometimes it seems to see itself as a continent on its own. As for its relationship with its neighbors, there is some rivalry with Argentina, which is easy to spot at any football match between the two national teams! Relations between Brazil and the other South American countries are changing, though, from rivalry to cooperation, thanks to special economic arrangements with the member states of the Southern Economic Area (Mercosul) and closer links within the Latin American community.

The size of the country appears to influence other situations as well. Brazilians like to talk about how

vast their forests are, how long their rivers, and the fact that you can encounter all types of climate and vegetation when traveling around Brazil. They also like to "think big," appreciating big plans and big ideas, such as the construction of the Itaipú dam or the city of Brasília. Not all the big projects are so successful, though. The half-built Transamazônica highway, which was intended to cross the Amazon region, connecting it to the rest of the country, was a total failure because it did not take environmental conditions into account.

NOVELAS AND FAVELAS

In Brazilian shantytowns, or *favelas*, you can find people living in total poverty, sometimes with all the members of an extended family sharing only one room. It tends to surprise outsiders that many of these houses have precarious basic sanitation, but they all have a TV set.

One of the things that unifies Brazilians from all regions and social classes is their passion for TV

soap operas, or *novelas*. They arouse a kind of national devotion that may even be compared to the Brazilian love of football. Although football is more male and *novelas* are more female oriented, family members of all ages sit in front of their TVs in the evenings to watch their favorites. The episodes are daily, Monday to Saturday.

Inspired by the American originals, both radio and television, the Latin American *telenovelas* introduced a major difference to the genre: they end (the story can last from three months to up to a year). Nowadays Brazilian *novelas* have a distinct identity and give an insight into the way people think and live. The Brazilian *novela* structure is based on three parallel plots, with characters who belong to the upper class, the middle class, and the lower class. The storylines cross over, so that there are relationships between plots and classes, reflecting the intermixing of social classes within Brazil, as well as providing everyone with characters they can identify with. The settings favor cities, particularly Rio.

Brazilian *novelas* can vary in imagination and scope in a way that soap operas in English-speaking countries never do: from historical pieces, adaptations of literature, or "imitation-of reality" to those that explore comedy, political farce, swashbuckling, surrealism, and even venture into magical realism, science fiction, and fantasy.

Commentators have claimed that television, through its *novelas*, is a fundamental force for Brazil's national integration, and partially responsible for the urbanization of the national culture. Furthermore, television reaches 97 percent of the 5,565 Brazilian cities, towns, and villages, and there has been the odd  occasion when the last episode of a particularly popular *novela* achieved over 90 percent of the audience. So people in an apartment in downtown São Paulo have been watching the same TV show as those in a hut in the middle of the rain forest.

TV critics complain that *novelas* alienate the majority of their audience by reproducing the values of the dominant classes, and to outsiders they may appear melodramatic and overemotional. Although that may be true, they often discuss social issues, including taboos, which would not normally be discussed in any other forum.

THE COUNTRY OF TOMORROW

Brazilians are mainly optimistic, even though sometimes this can come to mean that they have a passive attitude to life. Sayings such as "Everything works out in the end" (*Tudo dá certo no final*) place hopes for the future in the hands of fate rather than on individual actions. There is a belief that the future will provide and "Things will get better tomorrow" (*Amanhã tudo se resolve*).

In political terms, this oddly passive optimism might have been reinforced by past government propaganda proclaiming that "Brazil is the country of tomorrow." This meant that given Brazil's abundance of arable land and natural resources, it was just a matter of time before it became a key economic power. When Brazil became the sixth largest economy in the world, some incredulous citizens wondered whether tomorrow had finally arrived. Once it became apparent that achieving developed country status was easier said than done, critics answered this by saying "tomorrow is always tomorrow."

Short-Termism

Maybe because of this sense that it is fate and not rigorous planning that brings better days, Brazilians are not enthusiastic advocates of long-term projects. The short-termism mentality applies to business, political matters, collective memory, and personal life alike. For example, when a new business venture is started, return on capital investment is expected almost immediately.

Living for the Moment

It sometimes amazes foreigners how present-time based Brazilians are. They might organize a party for later the same day, or go out but decide where to go only when they are already on the move. Forward planning does not apply to much of social life, except on a few special occasions.

An outsider can be misled into thinking that living for the moment means that this is a carefree society, which is not exactly true. Brazilians, even without a lot of planning ahead, do worry about the future. It is just not so noticeable at first.

FOCUS ON RELATIONSHIPS

This is a relationship-focused and not system-oriented society. Together with the sense of immediacy, this means that, in both personal and business life, contacts are made face-to-face rather than through written communication. Phone calls are considerably lengthy, too. Time is spent on establishing and maintaining relationships. In business good personal contacts are important because, given the choice, Brazilians put people they know first and, if necessary, even bend the rules to accommodate their needs.

JEITINHO BRASILEIRO

The *jeitinho* is the Brazilian means of dealing creatively with life's everyday complications. Literally translated as "a little way," it can be taken to mean "there has to be another way." In practice, it means that regardless of the rules or systems in place, where there is a will there has to be a way around them. If you take the country's maddening bureaucracy and add the Brazilian tendency to challenge authority, you will understand how it comes to exist.

The *jeitinho* is so ingrained in daily life that you can see examples everywhere: managing to get a seat when all the places are booked up, traveling with more luggage than is allowed, or successfully ordering something that is not on the restaurant menu. Even in legal matters, if someone wants something that is not permitted, he or she will try to figure out a loophole until they find an alternative way.

Everyone for Themselves

The historical lack of social welfare is partly the reason for the high level of individualism in Brazilian society. Everyone has to fend for themselves and do the best they can. If that means having to go over other people's heads or take advantage of certain situations, some will choose to do so. Therefore, doing things like using a *jeitinho* to pay less tax (justified, perhaps, by saying that politicians misuse taxpayers' money) becomes what many consider to be an acceptable practice.

FAMILY TIES

Brazilian families are very closely knit. Since state support is small and reserved for the very poor, family members tend to help each other, sharing the good and the bad moments as they come. It is common for grandparents to help look after their grandchildren, for parents to provide for children no longer living with them, or for sons and daughters to give their parents a regular income when necessary. Family comes first and there are very many family businesses. Family rituals are important, too, including the family gathering for lunch at the weekend.

Father Figure

Although there are a number of women in positions of power in business, and in spite of women occupying important political positions, including the presidency of the country, Brazil is still a male-dominated society. Generally speaking, most Brazilians, particularly the less well educated, feel the need for a father figure, be it at work, in politics, or in religion. "God is father," as they say, and no, it is not a coincidence that paternalistic politicians tend to win elections. Curiously, the idea of paternalistic behavior being always negative does not apply in Brazil in the same way as in English-speaking countries. Be aware that what would be seen as patronizing in the UK or America could frequently be taken as simple advice or a demonstration of care by a Brazilian.

KNOWING YOUR PLACE

There is a conflict of ideologies when it comes to social mobility in Brazilian society. There is a sense that people should "know their place." For example, employees who belong to the lower, dominated classes should not try to "be something more than they are." This feeling has its roots in the colonial past and is still strong in rural areas, especially in those places that grew up around sugar plantations, such as in the Northeast.

In the larger centers there is more of a "can do" attitude, a belief that it is possible to climb the social ladder via personal effort. This is not unlike the attitude found in many parts of the USA and, similarly, it stems from the experience of immigrants forging new lives in a new land.

FORMAL OR INFORMAL?

Brazilians are usually informal in the way they dress, talk, and approach new friendships, or when making decisions. However, older people are addressed by the title *Seu* (Mr.), *Dona* (Ms.), or even *Doutor(a)* (Dr.)—even for people who have no academic title and are not in the medical profession—before their first names (for example, Seu Daniel, Dona Alice, Doutora Ana). Moreover, when using any type of formal address, Brazilians have a deferential form of "you" that is used in the third person (*o senhor/a senhora* followed by the verb in the third person), similar to a waiter asking in English "What does sir require?"

Even though the approach to many matters may be extremely informal, Brazil is a class-based culture and places importance on everything denoting power, social class, or material wealth.

LOOKING GOOD

There is a Brazilian saying: "The world treats people better when they dress well" (*o mundo trata melhor quem se veste bem*). Brazilians care a good deal about appearances and not simply about what to wear. You are what you appear to be, so everyone should do their best to look as attractive, young, and fit as they can. Individuals of all ages care for their bodies as much for vanity's sake as for health reasons and the middle classes exercise in gyms, in parks, and on beaches. Most women and some men dye their hair. It is not a coincidence that Brazil has some of the best plastic surgeons in the world: they get a lot of practice. This is a country that loves beauty in nature, in architecture, and in people. A famous Brazilian poet once said "May the ugly excuse me, but beauty is fundamental" (*As feias que me desculpem mas beleza é fundamental*).

AGEISM

Despite reports about the drop in the birth rate, Brazil is a young country with a strong youth culture. It is no surprise that people will go to great lengths to look as youthful as they can. From fashion to TV shows, it seems that everything is targeted at the under thirties. It is almost as if it is bad manners to become old. In employment terms, this means that it may be harder for someone over forty, and certainly over fifty, to find a new job.

SQUEAKY CLEAN

The expression "cleanliness is next to godliness" could have been written about Brazilians. While it is true that the streets are not always pristine, and that in *favelas* without basic sanitation you can smell the poverty, individuals from all walks of life set great store by personal hygiene.

Showers are often long and frequent. People tend to shower and change before going out. Similarly, a shower is important before going to bed. Brazilians generally brush their teeth before breakfast and after eating any meal.

BETTER LATE THAN NEVER

Brazilians find it hard to organize their own time and schedule their day around fixed points. This could be due to an influence from the indigenous peoples, in whose culture the notion of punctuality does not exist. Whatever the reason, Brazilians struggle to be on time. Being late is part of their culture and whoever deals with them should remember that. The degree of lateness may vary according to the region, but it will always be a feature.

SAUDADE

You cannot talk about the Brazilian soul without mentioning *saudade*. Although it is normally explained as nostalgia or the sense of missing something, there is no actual translation for this term in English that takes account of its references to the local culture.

Saudade is what you feel when someone you love is away or is unattainable, or when an event has slipped into the past, but in either case you feel happy to cherish the memories. It is a mix of nostalgia, melancholy, longing, desire, a bit of sadness but happiness too, because when you feel *saudade*, the things, moments, or people you have feelings about will be with you in your mind. *Saudade* is more than an emotional response to a memory, it is an inspirational feeling that Brazilians actively seek and thrive on. It is not by chance that many popular songs, be they sad or happy, mention the word *saudade*.

GREEN AND YELLOW

Brazilians have an interesting relationship with the symbols of their country. Wearing the colors of the national flag, green and yellow, is supposed to be in bad taste unless the occasion is a *Carnaval* or a football match.

Colloquially, someone is said to be *bandeiroso* (flaggy) or *dando bandeira* (giving away a flag) when behaving inappropriately or showing off.

Social scientists have claimed that this was in fact a reaction to the political system during the military dictatorship, which expropriated the country's national symbols. At this time, the use of the flag was actually forbidden unless at a civic occasion, such as a national football match. In any case, the flag could not be printed on T-shirts or similar items. Many things have changed since, and the prohibition on the use of the Brazilian flag has been abolished. The result has been an immense quantity of flag printed T-shirts, caps, thongs, and bags invading the shops.

Brazilians still avoid wearing the colors green and yellow together, though.

PRIDE AND PREJUDICE

For a country that claims to have a "racial democracy," the treatment of different ethnic groups is not always very egalitarian. Brazilians with fair skin, light-colored eyes, and surnames that are difficult to pronounce are already halfway there when fighting for a better job. Also, those who consider themselves white will be offended if referred to as mixed race, even if they actually are.

As a reaction to such "white pride," members of Brazil's black movement have been successful in promoting black music and culture. But most dark-skinned Brazilians also come from the poorest sectors of society, so even when they can escape the (veiled) racial prejudice, they still face some economic barriers.

HAPPY TO BE BRAZILIANS

Despite complaining about their country, government, and weather (!) all the time, there are several songs about being Brazilian, and they are decidedly positive. In spite of it all, Brazilians seem to enjoy the particularities of their culture. They may grumble about everything and everybody, but in the end they are simply happy to be Brazilians.

But beware: while Brazilians can be highly critical of certain aspects of their country—

especially bureaucracy, the social system, and politics—even moderate criticism is not so welcome when coming from outsiders.

WHAT'S NEW?

Brazil is a relatively young country. It is thus not surprising that it is attracted to the new, but very few nations are as open to it as Brazil. This attitude seems to have started early, during the period of colonization.

It has been said that Brazil was a country where foreigners could change their destiny without losing their identity. Even if their original identity remained, however, something would certainly have been added to it. The early marriages between Europeans and Native Indians must have given rise to huge culture shock. Newcomers continue to be attracted by the Brazilians' tolerance of racial mixture and the resulting cultural flexibility, particularly in the big cities. It is an open-mindedness that extends to other areas, such as sexuality or business practices. Brazil is thirsty for fresh, original ideas and is so accustomed to these that, maybe, it really can absorb new cultures, or businesses, without being afraid that its own identity will be affected.

chapter three

RELIGION, CUSTOMS, & TRADITIONS

GOD IS EVERYWHERE

According to a popular saying, "God is Brazilian." Leaving discussions about His nationality aside, what is undeniably true is that God is everywhere in Brazil. Brazilians are a deeply religious people and there are many different faiths practiced within the country. Even outside formalized observance there is an affinity with the spiritual and supernatural sides of life and the influences of religion, superstition, and mysticism are so great that they affect even nonbelievers.

In spite of having the largest Catholic population of any country, the number of Catholics has dropped (from 80 percent to 65 percent in 2010) and there has been a significant rise in the Evangelical movement (22 percent). Brazilians may also attend the ceremonies of other faiths. The practice of various cults incorporating African and Native Indian beliefs, sometimes condoned by the Church, is popular, widespread, and socially accepted.

THE CATHOLIC CHURCH AND THE STATE

Brazil was officially Catholic from the arrival of the Portuguese until the end of the monarchy. During these four centuries, the practice of any other religion was illegal. But colonization was concentrated on the coast, and the institutions of the state and Church were centralized in the capital. So, in practice, due to the very small number of priests, their power and control were limited to those areas. Even so, the Inquisition— the official ecclesiastical tribunal for the suppression of heresy—warned of African influences on the beliefs of Brazilian Catholics.

The African slaves, since they had been forbidden to follow their own religions, disguised their deities by identifying them with Catholic saints and worshiping them in this form. This fooled the Portuguese into believing they had converted. The Native Indians, on the other hand, welcomed the Catholic saints and worshiped them alongside the spirits of the forest.

Since the founding of the republic, Church and state have remained separate. Although the dominant religion is Roman Catholicism, in 1988 only 17 percent of those calling themselves Catholic regularly attended Sunday mass. As well as the recognized world faiths, Brazil is also home to a number of hybrid religions, born out of the merging of indigenous and African beliefs with Catholicism. The Church does not accept nor recognize these faiths.

The relationship between Church and state has had its ups and downs. Although no longer the official religion, Catholicism has had a strong influence on political decisions. It largely supported the state until the time of the dictatorship, when sections of the Church broke away. Even now it lobbies members of the legislature and manages to block the promotion of certain policies. Abortion, for example, is still illegal in Brazil.

The liturgical calendar guides the devotion of the country's Catholics and is followed by all other Christian denominations.

AFRICAN AND NATIVE INFLUENCED RELIGIONS
Candomblé
Candomblé started as a unique Brazilian mixture of rites from different African religions. Its rituals and myths stress the ancestral memories of Africa but not the history of African slaves in Brazil.

The religious syncretism of Candomblé meant that each of the originally African divinities

(*orixás*) corresponded to a Catholic saint. This structure, along with the party-like style of the ceremonies, attracted black and white followers alike, from the poorer classes to the social elite, and became particularly popular among artists. Today it is possible to find Candomblé adherents even among Brazilian Jews and Japanese. The celebration of the *orixás* has also been exported to the neighboring country of Argentina.

In the ceremonies, the *orixás* manifest themselves through mediums. Not preaching but dancing, they establish a relationship with a cosmic dimension that bridges mythical times and present-day life. The mediums dress ceremonially and observe a strict and solemn ritual with specific gestures marked by chanting and drumming. Like any social gathering, it all ends with a meal, when everybody eats the sacred food that has been offered to the *orixás*.

Candomblé seems to be the Afro-Brazilian religion that has kept most of the African traditions intact. Despite using the images of Catholic saints, it has managed to preserve the characteristics of the *orixás* and their elaborate rituals. In some Candomblé houses, the original names and images of the *orixás* have been reinstated (displacing the Catholic ones), attracting the interest of Africans who want to learn about their own religions as it was practiced by their ancestors.

Pajelança

The *pajés*, or shamans, play a fundamental role in

caboclo culture (see Chapter 1, Regions, page 17), especially in areas with a strong indigenous culture. They offer spiritual guidance and act as healers. The use of local plants and the ability to mingle their therapeutic and magic qualities is one

of the *pajés'* sacred secrets. They reach a state of connection with the "essence" of the forest and communicate with the spirit world through a mystical trance. The ceremonies include singing, dancing, and miming the qualities of the supernatural forces they want to invoke, normally spirits of animals, natural elements, or long dead ancestors.

Some *pajés* consider themselves Catholics, and this segment of Pajelança is called Encantaria. The lack of recognition by the Church does not stop Encantaria's followers from worshiping Catholic saints, which is also combined with respect for the "enchanted ones," spiritual beings from the forest.

Pajelança rituals vary from region to region and inside and outside the various tribes. In the more urban areas its rites are combined with elements from Afro-Brazilian religions and Spiritualism.

Umbanda

Umbanda originated as a combination of Candomblé and Spiritualism (see page 76, below). However, Umbanda mythology has its own set of divinities, divided into seven hierarchical "lines," each of them led by a Catholic saint or an *orixá*. As well as having a strict hierarchy, Umbanda features a cast of characters commonly considered marginal to society. The array of entities or "guides" includes *pretos velhos* (old black slaves), *caboclos* from the forest, *exus* (mischievous spirits), *pomba-giras* (streetwise women), and the spirits of children. What binds them together is that they all possess realistic wisdom from every walk of  life. In this way they can understand and help with any sort of everyday conflict. The main altar is decorated with images of Christ, Our Lady, Catholic saints, *orixás*, *caboclos*, *pretos velhos*, candles, flowers, and sometimes a Brazilian flag (Umbanda followers see theirs as a patriotic religion).

Quimbanda

Also called Macumba, this has a similar belief system to Umbanda, but it explores the ambivalence between good and evil. A very simplistic description could say that Quimbanda "works for evil," while Umbanda is supposed to "work for

good." The two cults share the idea of a cosmos separated into two realms that can be accessed through a series of spiritual spells and counterspells.

KARDECISM (SPIRITUALISM)

Spiritualism in Brazil was inspired by the ideas of nineteenth-century French mystic Allan Kardec (1804–69), and combines positivism and mysticism via the services of a medium. Kardec's doctrine had such a positive response here that in the twentieth century Brazil became the country where Spiritualism was most widely practiced, particularly among the middle classes. Kardecist spiritualists believe in reincarnation, and set great store on charitable deeds. Mediums guide the spirits of the departed to a more elevated plane of existence.

Most of the Portuguese-language literature on this religious sect was "psychowritten" by the medium Chico Xavier (1910–2002), who became a best-selling author in Brazil.

PROTESTANTS

It would be a mistake to group all Brazil's different Protestant denominations together under the same banner. They vary in their style of worship and clerical structure as well as in their origins. Protestant missionaries went to Brazil in the nineteenth century, while Lutheran pastors and Anglican vicars arrived along with the German and English communities, followed by Swedish missionaries. Presbyterians, Methodists, Mormons, Baptists, and Seventh Day Adventists have all found fertile territory in which to expand their influence. Indeed, the increase in the number of Evangelical and Pentecostal converts is a phenomenon of national significance, mainly among the poorer classes.

Brazil's Universal Church of the Kingdom of God, one of the most vocal congregations (it owns a large national TV network), has even expanded overseas, with branches in the USA, the UK, and other European countries. Its members are inspired by the Holy Spirit, calling on people to be guided only by Jesus Christ. In Brazilian religious terms, this implies turning their back not only on the idolatrous images of the Catholic saints, but also on a multitude of entities and divinities of mixed origins, and adopting a consistent puritanical lifestyle.

THIRD-MILLENNIUM RELIGIONS

The followers of these cults combine Ufology with Spiritualism, and believe in the dawn of a new civilization. They support the unification of all religions moved by universal love. Their temples are based around the city of Brasília, "the capital of the third millennium." The main one, Templo da Boa Vontade (Temple of Goodwill) has the shape of a seven-sided pyramid with a massive crystal at its summit and a vast meditation area.

Religion is both fertile and fluid in Brazil. The differences, particularly between Afro-Brazilian cults, are sometimes academic. In practice, the myths tend to blend into one another, giving birth to new cults, even if they keep their original denominations.

Other religions in Brazil include Judaism, Islam, Buddhism, the Japanese "Messianica" and Seicho-no-ie. There is also a growing number of eastern inspired forms of meditation practice.

SUPERSTITIONS

With such a rich collection of religions and mythologies, it is understandable that Brazilians are superstitious.

Superstitious ritual behavior is part of the daily life of believers and nonbelievers alike. It is not uncommon to find an atheist who takes the ideas of "bad vibes" and the "evil eye" for real. But there is no reason to fear: knock on wood, and the evil will go away.

FOOTBALL: THE UNIFYING RELIGION

Football (that is, soccer) can be seen as the "cult" that brings together Brazilians from all belief systems. The passion it inspires in the people can certainly be compared to religious devotion. In fact, Catholics, Evangelicals, and followers of all different cults pray in the hope that this will help their team to victory. Brazilian football players even make the sign of the cross when they run on to the football pitch. However, it is the grace and artistry of Brazilian players that really moves their supporters.

Football was brought to Brazil by the English and soon became a national passion, played all over the country—even by some indigenous tribes. It has become widely acknowledged that the way Brazilian football is played is something special. Comments have been made about the skill, balance, and grace of the Brazilian national team down through the generations. The Brazilian game seems to have been influenced by the movements and dances of African origin, such as *samba* and *capoeira* (a dance game created by black slaves to disguise the practice of foot fighting). Football attracts many players from disadvantaged backgrounds. In a country with such an unequal distribution of wealth and access to good quality education, football has become one of the few ways to rise up the social ladder.

Brazil is the only country to have won five World Cups, and the fortunes of its national team impact directly and significantly on its citizens. When it wins, everybody joins in the general climate of ecstasy.

Some stores even shut their doors to take part in the celebrations, and the mood is just like *Carnaval*.

A national holiday was declared when Brazil won the World Cup for the fifth time. This was probably a wise move as shops and offices were likely to have been deserted anyway. On the other hand, when the team loses, people can be seen crying openly as they leave the grounds and there is a tangible and widespread feeling of sadness.

Such occurrences are not confined to the World Cup. When there is a local derby between two major teams, the streets are empty and people are glued to a TV set anywhere they can find one. The tension is broken only by roars of celebration and the sound of fireworks when a team scores and commentators scream "gooooaaaaaaal!!!" for as long as they can.

BRAZILIAN NATIONAL HOLIDAYS

DATE	FESTIVAL
January 1	New Year
February/March	*Carnaval*
March/April	Good Friday
April 21	Tiradentes
May 1	Labor Day
May/June	Corpus Christi
September 7	Independence Day
October 12	*Nossa Senhora Aparecida* (patron saint of Brazil)
November 2	All Souls
November 15	Proclamation of the Republic
December 25	Christmas

OTHER CELEBRATIONS	
April 19	*Dia do Índio* (Indigenous Peoples' Day)
June 12	*Dia dos Namorados* (Beloved's Day)
June 13, 24, and 29	*Festas Juninas* (June Parties)

THE FESTIVE CALENDAR

Brazil used to have a lengthy list of national holidays, mainly based around Catholic festivals. Nowadays, after complaints from employers and successive governmental changes, just a few remain. States and municipalities can use their discretion to add holidays to the national calendar, though. They might decide to keep a religious holiday that has been nationally abolished, or they might take a day off to celebrate the foundation of their city or commemorate its patron saint.

Depending on the day, Brazilians will tend to "extend" their holiday. If the holiday falls on a Tuesday, some might take the Monday off. If it falls on Thursday, many will not work on Friday. This applies particularly to public institutions, such as schools, and all sorts of bureaucratic services. In the big cities, though, one can always find places like shopping malls that never seem to close their doors.

New Year—January 1

For a spiritual, optimistic nation, New Year is just the time to prepare for a new beginning. New Year's

Eve is marked by preparations for the evening party. Most people wear white and sometimes give each other little tokens to bring luck: something white will bring peace, something yellow riches, and so on. A few will also wear a piece of colored underwear according to the "wish" they make. A midnight feast among family and friends is the usual way to start the New Year. Others may go to the beach.

Followers of Afro-Brazilian religions have a special ritual in which they make offerings, generally flowers, to the goddess of the sea, Iemanjá. She is the wife of Oxalá, the god who personifies

heaven, and the mother of all *orixás*. Under the system of religious syncretism, Iemanjá is also associated with Our Lady the Holy Virgin. In the spirit of all things Brazilian, some nonbelievers go to watch the ceremonies and end up throwing a few flowers onto the sea, just in case. Anyhow, the beach is the main destination for those who decide to go out on the last day of the year, if not for the offering of flowers, then certainly for the firework displays in the main coastal cities.

Carnaval—February/March
Carnaval, together with football, is the most significant demonstration of popular culture in

Brazil. Its importance is so great that Brazilians themselves divide the annual calendar into before and after *Carnaval*. As a matter of fact, they say that nothing functions and the year does not start until the end of the *Carnaval* period. If you have to do any work or arrange any meetings at the beginning of the year in Brazil, you might very well find this to be true.

Carnaval takes place on the four days before Ash Wednesday and was originally supposed to be the final time of self-indulgence before Lent, the forty-day period of austerity and abstinence leading to Easter. However, the festival seems to have earlier roots in Roman ceremonies to honor the deity Saturn (who was associated with seed corn and sowing), which also involved the worship of Bacchus, the god of wine. During the festivities, the traditional order of Roman society was set aside and slaves and masters shared the same public space. The early Church disapproved of these "bacchanalias" and restricted them to the period prior to Lent.

In Brazil the four days of *Carnaval* are a mixture of partying, dance spectacle, folklore, and art. The whole country stops and people of all ages and social backgrounds share the joy. It is a magical time when social conventions are ignored or turned upside down. The poor can dress up in luxurious costumes and become royalty. The rich turn into pirates or Native Indians. Men can turn into women and women can wear as little as they wish. People may steal kisses, flirt, drink, and dance through the night and the following day until it is night once more. It is a nonstop game of make-believe, where anyone can escape into a fantasy world and be whoever and do whatever they feel like. At least, this is what they think.

Carnaval takes over the big cities and small towns alike. Every community has its own traditional way of celebrating, but there are two

spaces where it usually takes place: on the street and in private clubs. The street is given over to parades and dancing, while in the clubs you will find anything from updated bacchanalias to well-behaved, family-oriented balls. The most famous *Carnavals* take place in Rio de Janeiro, Salvador, and Olinda/Recife.

Rio

The Rio *Carnaval* is the biggest in the country. It attracts the most tourists and its organization has influenced all other *Carnavals* based around competing samba schools. Participants work the whole year to make the costumes they wear in the big parade. Various samba schools take part in the parade and are judged by a panel of artists, musicians, and intellectuals. The choice of the winner is based on the creativity and success of the costumes, the enthusiasm of the participants of the subdivisions (*alas*), the movements of the dance,

and the music. A fundamental element is the *samba-enredo*: the theme of this song inspires all the costumes and allegories used by the samba school. The parade lasts all through *Carnaval* and takes place in the Sambódromo, a building specially designed by architect Oscar Niemeyer to help create a dreamlike feeling. Discussions about the samba school performances hijack the news and take over the TV programming. Some have become disillusioned by the hype and feel that the Rio *Carnaval* has actually turned into a TV show.

Salvador

Despite scholars saying that samba was born in the state of Bahia, the biggest part of the *Carnaval* in Salvador is not based on it. Here celebrations center around the Trio Elétrico. This started when a couple of musicians, during *Carnaval*, decided to play the traditionally acoustic rhythm of *frevo* using electric instruments on top of their car. They invited a guest musician along and called themselves the Trio Elétrico. Now, instead of a car, huge trucks with "*axé* music" bands on top parade through the streets of Salvador, attracting a multitude of people who follow them around, dancing. "*Axé* music" is a mixture of African rhythms with pop music. The most famous Trios Elétricos attract about 4,000 followers and parade for hours nonstop.

Recife and Olinda
Recife wakes up early on Saturday to usher in the festivities on the first day of *Carnaval*. Massive numbers of people go to watch and follow the carnival parade of *Galo da Madrugada* (Dawn Cockerel).

In neighboring Olinda, giant puppets fill the hills of the city in an amazing street carnival, accompanied by the sounds of *frevo*. The mornings cater more to children and older people, with great displays of improvisation and imagination. *Foliões* (carnival dancers) make up last-minute outfits and have as much fun as others who obviously spend a great deal of time preparing more elaborate costumes. Improvisation is also a feature of the carnival *blocos* (groups). Some *blocos* are traditional and long-established, but new groups are invented every *Carnaval* and anyone can have a go. Apart from *frevo*, people also dance to the rhythm of *caboclinho*s, music of indigenous origin. Possibly the most beautiful moment of this carnival is *A Noite dos Tambores Silenciosos* (The Night of the Silent Drums) on *Carnaval* Monday in Recife city center. Different groups of *maracatú*, performing what was originally a religious dance from the sugar plantation areas, meet in front of the Nossa Senhora do Rosário dos Pretos Church to reenact a two-hundred-year-old slave ceremony. The drums stop playing at midnight, the lights go off, and everybody observes a minute of silence, after which the players call for the black gods in African languages, followed by chanting and drumming.

These are just the most famous *Carnaval* highlights. Unfortunately, because they are the best known they also draw a large number of visitors, compromising part of the spontaneity of the festival.

Good Friday—March/April

This is the only official day off work during Easter, although this varies according to region. In the big cities, *Sexta-Feira da Paixão*, as it is called, is just a day when you can find fish on all the restaurant menus (because of the Catholic restriction on meat on that day). In smaller, more religious communities there may be special masses, processions, musical concerts, and sacred art exhibitions. The most spectacular of all celebrations has to be the dramatization of the Passion of Christ in Brejo da Madre de Deus, near Caruaru, in inland Pernambuco. The small town has only one hotel, plus a few B&Bs, and its size does not prepare any outsider for what they are about to witness.

The *Paixão de Cristo* takes place in the "theater city" of Nova Jerusalém (New Jerusalem), enclosed by high stone walls, with seven towers and doors. It is said that the actual area of the "theater city" is one-third of that of the Old City in Jerusalem. Inside it, around five hundred actors reenact the Passion of Christ on twelve open stages. The audience join in and become "extras," and follow the actors through sixty scenes from one set to the next, in a "mobile theater" experience. This spectacle used to be performed by local actors for a regional audience. Its fame has grown since professional actors have joined in. It now attracts visitors from different parts of the country, but rarely foreigners.

Dia do Índio **(Indigenous Peoples' Day)—April 19**
The *Dia do Índio* is commemorated in every school in the country. It tends to be an opportunity for youngsters and artists to talk about indigenous culture and for the indigenous people to organize protests.

Tiradentes—April 21
The first conspiracy against the Portuguese government was hatched in 1789, in today's city

of Ouro Preto, Minas Gerais. At the time it was a prosperous gold-mining center, and a few young intellectuals from wealthy families, inspired by the ideas of the American Revolution and French Enlightenment philosophers, got together to discuss the increasing economic exploitation by Portugal.

Left alone, their discussions would probably not have amounted to anything, but the government needed to demonstrate strength and used the conspirators as examples. Tiradentes, the leader, was hanged, becoming the first Brazilian political martyr. The date is remembered as the first demonstration of a separate Brazilian identity.

Labor Day—May 1
This is a national holiday.

Corpus Christi—May/June
This Catholic feast day celebrating the gift of the Holy Eucharist falls on the eighth week after Easter Sunday. It is one of the few remaining ecclesiastical holidays.

Dia dos Namorados (Beloved's Day)—June 12
This is not a national holiday as such but the date is certainly kept across the whole country. A bit like a Brazilian version of Valentine's Day, on the *Dia dos Namorados* people will give a gift to their girlfriends or boyfriends. Lovers, partners, and married couples are all reminded of the date by shop windows everywhere. Fathers tend to buy their daughters a little gift as well.

Festas Juninas (June Parties)

The June Parties take different forms in each region. They are meant to honor the Catholic Saints Anthony, Paul, John, and Peter.

St. Anthony's Day is celebrated on June 13. Brazilians consider him to be the patron saint of marriages, helping single women who are looking for a husband. Unmarried women may light candles and offer flowers to his image, but if that doesn't result in a boyfriend some persuasion might be required. In the interior, where these traditions are still alive, spinsters "torture" the image of the saint, hanging it upside down or "drowning" it in a bowl of water. If this produces a marriage, the saint might even get an altar to himself. The *Dia dos Namorados* (St. Valentine's Day) was established on June 12 because it was the day before St. Anthony's Day, as part of the same celebration.

St. Peter's Day is June 29, but in the Northeast most parties are dedicated to St. John the Baptist on June 24. There, São João is the biggest street party after *Carnaval*. Northeasterners decorate their houses and streets with flags, cook peanut and sweet-corn based foods, and dance the *forró* (an upbeat rhythm from the interior) all night.

Toward the south, every school has its own June party. Local churches also organize June parties almost every weekend. In the Quermesse, they play games, very much like those at summer fairs, and dance the *quadrilha* (square dance) around a bonfire. People eat food made of sweet potatoes and nuts, especially peanuts, although more recently there has been the addition of hot dogs and popcorn. They also drink mulled wine and *quentão*, an alcoholic beverage made out of ginger, to warm them on the winter evenings.

Independence Day—September 7
Schoolchildren and the military have parades on this day.

Nossa Senhora Aparecida **(the patron saint of Brazil)—October 12**
Literally "Our Lady Who Appeared," *Nossa Senhora Aparecida* became Brazil's patron saint when, in 1717, a fisherman found a ceramic image of a black Madonna. Soon miracles started to happen in connection with this Madonna and the news about Her powers spread throughout the nation. Her church is situated in Aparecida do Norte, a small town between São Paulo and Rio de Janeiro, and it is visited by more than three million people a year.

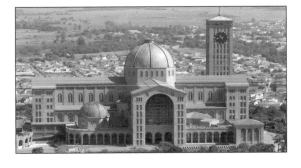

All Souls—November 2
All Souls, or *Dia de Finados* (literally, Day of the Dead), is a festival dedicated to remembering loved

ones who have passed away. Many Brazilians go to the cemeteries to take flowers to the tombs of their relatives. In some cities special buses are organized to help people reach the cemeteries.

Proclamation of the Republic—November 15
In election years, the date of the proclamation of the republic is chosen to be polling day. As the elections for mayors, members of parliament, and presidents occur in different years, this civic holiday is almost always taken up by everybody lining up to vote for their chosen candidates.

Christmas—December 25
For people from countries where Christmas is the main holiday, the Brazilian version may be a bit of a disappointment. Despite the heat (it occurs during summer) there are still Santas in shops, particularly in those with air-conditioning.

Christmas is mainly a family celebration, and since the Brazilian concept of family extends beyond parents and their offspring it tends to be a big event with children running around. Although the national holiday is on December 25, the main celebration is on Christmas Eve, with a midnight feast and exchange of gifts. Brazilians do not care for cards but are big on presents, buying them for all their friends and relatives. These will also include the postman, the porter of their building, their house cleaner, and work colleagues. The idea of Christmas gifts for all is so ingrained that all employed people receive a "thirteenth salary," an extra month's pay, during the festive season.

LOCAL FESTIVALS

Lavagem do Bonfim—Second Thursday in January

The ritual called the Washing of Bonfim takes place only in Salvador, Bahia, but it may very well be the most important ceremony for Candomblé followers. The festival consists of a long procession of about 800,000 people dressed in white. It ends in front of the Church of Nosso Senhor do Bonfim (Our Lord of Good Endings), where the faithful perform a ritual washing of the steps that lead to the church. This is a clear indication of the degree of syncretism and religious tolerance in Brazil. The church is considered a sacred place in Candomblé—Our Lord of Bonfim is associated with the divinity Oxalá, father of the *orixás* and creator of humankind.

Salvador is the spiritual center of Candomblé and holds several of its festivals, some coinciding with Catholic saints' days.

Parintins Folklore Festival—June

The Parintins Folklore Festival takes place throughout most of the month of June and consists of a series of indigenous shows and ritual dramatizations. Indigenous music marks every event in a festival that is for the North what *Carnaval* is for the rest of Brazil.

Parintins, in the state of Amazonas, is a small island in the middle of the Amazon River. To get there people catch the boat in Manaus for a trip that takes at least twenty-four hours, and many spend the nights on board since Parintins does not have accommodation for many visitors.

All the Amazon states share the tradition of *Boi-bumbá* or *Bumba meu boi* presentations during the June festivities. The *bumba* is a popular dance and, although the theme might vary, the basic story recounts the adventures of a slave who kills his boss's ox because his pregnant wife wishes to eat cow's tongue. The slave owner finds out. To escape his anger, the slave tries to bring the ox back to life . . . and he succeeds, at which moment everybody present shouts "*Bumba meu boi!*" ("Swing it, ox!").

The high point of the festival occurs at the end of the month, when two rival *bumba* groups, Garantido and Caprichoso, confront each other, the winner being the one that provokes the best reactions from the audience.

Círio de Nazaré (Candles of Nazareth)—October

This is one of the largest Catholic festivals,

attracting around two million people to Belém in the state of Pará for two weeks starting on the second Sunday of October. In 1700 someone found a statue of Our Lady lying by an *igarapé* (waterway) and took it home. To his surprise, the statue disappeared from his house and was found back where he had originally seen it. According to legend, this happened repeatedly, even when the state governor instructed it to be kept under guard. A church was built on the site where the statue was found, and the procession of the statue of Our Lady of Nazareth has been held since 1793. To illuminate the procession during the night, the faithful hold torches and sizable wax candles called *círios*.

Mãe Preta do Castainho (Castainho's Black Mother)—May

This is a party organized by the descendants of the community of Quilombo dos Palmares, the biggest and most successful community of runaway slaves, in the state of Pernambuco. The black slaves' descendants keep their ancestors' cultural traditions, as well as the collective work practices that they created in the past: 170 families produce sweet corn, beans, cassava, and flour, which is hand milled using their original equipment.

In the *Festa da Mãe Preta* (Party of the Black Mother), the oldest woman is chosen from the Castainho community to be that year's "black mother" and this is celebrated in music and dance.

This is just a small selection from the huge number of festivals that you can find in Brazil. There is also a whole host of cowboy festivals, agricultural festivals, festivals celebrating legends, and others that follow different cultural calendars from immigrant nations. These are still observed by their descendants . . . and everybody else in the neighborhood. Perhaps there is some truth to the cliché that Brazil is a nation that knows how to party. Another way of looking at it would be that Brazilians attach great importance to celebration.

chapter four

MAKING FRIENDS

Brazilians in general are very open and welcoming. Strangers can strike up conversations about politics and the weather waiting in line, on the beach, in the shops. A casual conversation in the supermarket can end up with an exchange of phone numbers. These signs can be misleading, though. Good friendships may very well start like this, but the fact is that while Brazilians are naturally sociable it takes far more to be admitted into their circle of friends.

MEETING PEOPLE

As in any other place, a good way to get to know people who have things in common with you is to enroll in an evening course, become a member of a club, or go to the gym.

Unprepared visitors might be surprised when hearing the comment "I'll come too" regarding rather dull activities they have planned and not really invited anyone to. Going to the post office or the pharmacist may not be a very appealing outing, but if you are enjoying someone's company you can carry on talking as you tag along. People often do things together. If they want to join a gym, for example, they will probably ask their friends if they

would like to too. So don't be surprised if your
Brazilian colleague comes to the supermarket
with you but leaves without buying a thing.

Brazilians do not restrict themselves to their
own age group when socializing or making friends.
Although school buddies might be of a similar age,
social groups are often made up of people from
any generation, and mutual interests and affinities
count more than years. Brazilians often go out
in groups, which tend to be very inclusive and
ever-expanding.

SOCIALIZING WITH WORK COLLEAGUES

There are various situations where one can meet
and socialize, but the most common is through the
workplace. People who work together certainly
make small talk, and sometimes have lunch

together. They discuss their families, hobbies, favorite movies, and the natural next step is to arrange something outside work. Singles socialize more after work than married people and have more flexibility for planning their weekends. Be aware, when arranging a dinner out with married friends, that they may bring the children along too.

In beach cities there is a culture of occasionally carrying on a work discussion in the bar after work. Refusing such an invitation could give the impression of someone who is not willing to commit and could well have a bearing on future employment. Maybe it is because the weather outside is more inviting than in the office, or maybe it is a subtle way of reconciling the fact that, although the working day is over, they have not finished everything they were supposed to. In either case, this does not count as overtime.

The city of São Paulo is the odd one out. Perhaps because it is such a big place, *paulistanos* tend to keep to themselves. They are less likely to strike up a casual conversation. They may take longer to invite you out from work, but when they do you are on the way to forming a friendship.

SOCIALIZING WITH THE OPPOSITE SEX

Carnaval and beach images have associated Brazilian women with tiny bikinis and sun-bronzed sensuality. But beach fashion only applies when one is on the beach, and the same can be said about *Carnaval*. Although sensuality is part of Brazilian culture, taking the stereotype as reality could not be a worse start.

Just like everything else, the way the opposite sexes socialize varies in different parts of the country. In the cities people of either sex go out together as regular friends. Much further inland, there are places where one should not address a married or engaged woman in case a jealous partner takes it personally and reacts violently.

Brazilians make an effort to look good and, while they may expect and be pleased to be complimented, such remarks stay at the level of appreciation only and do not tend to lead anywhere else.

As a general observation, Brazilians are tactile. Men tap each other on the shoulder. Women can touch each other's knees when they are sitting, as a way of emphasizing a point in the conversation. They may hold arms or hands as a demonstration of friendship. People from both sexes touch arms, shoulders, and hands as they are talking to each other. Such physical contact is part of Brazilian body language and should most definitely not be considered as anything other than that.

INVITATIONS HOME

Particularly in the larger urban centers, friends eat out more than at home, so being invited to someone's house is an invitation to share their private space and to be introduced to their family. You will be expected to take a small gift and something for the children, if appropriate. A present from your country would be appreciated (traditional handicraft, typical artwork, a coffee-table book, chocolate for the children), plus a bottle of wine or whiskey. Whatever you choose, avoid the colors purple and black, as some people identify them with mourning.

Strict punctuality is not expected on such occasions: about fifteen minutes after the time arranged would be just right. Dinner will probably not be served right away. The evening may start with informal drinks and aperitifs , normally in the living room.

You should not offer to help with the cooking, or, for that matter, help yourself to anything in the kitchen, unless invited to do so. The same goes for doing the dishes. Dinner is usually a relaxed affair and can end quite late. For Brazilians eating is a social thing.

FOREIGN FASCINATION

In a way, being a foreigner might ease first contacts in this culture. Brazilians are naturally curious and welcome most things from abroad. Outsiders bring

Reading It Right

Brazilians like to be seen as a nice and friendly people—and they generally are. But sometimes taking them literally may be the cause of a social gaffe. An Englishman who had recently arrived in the country made his first contacts in Brazil and was surprised to be received so openly. Eager to start a social life, he was happy when an acquaintance said he should come to their place sometime. Being English, he tried to arrange a day and time for visiting, but was told only "Turn up at any time." So he did. He could not hide his embarrassment when he realized they did not really mean it and he had completely misread their intention, which was similar to the American "Let's do lunch"—a polite way of keeping doors open to a possible relationship in the future. When people want to arrange something, they will mention a date.

new points of view, or at least they can appreciate Brazilian things from a different perspective.

There are expatriate communities, such as people who work in British Council offices or American Consulates, but they also socialize with Brazilians on a regular basis. These opportunities for cultural interchange seem to be too good to miss. However, someone can live in Brazil for a considerable time, lead a very sociable life, and still have no close friends there, because being considered a close friend is a substantial step-up.

FRIENDSHIP THE BRAZILIAN WAY

As well as the closeness of the family network, and the love invested in it, Brazilians set great store by close friendships. To be a friend is both a privilege and a responsibility. Friends have each other's best interests in mind. A friend is someone you celebrate with when something good comes your way. It is also someone you can rely on when bad things happen.

For people from cultures where you are supposed to be all right on your own and where private space is to be respected, the idea of Brazilian friendship may seem quite invasive.

For a start, there are no off-limit conversations. Moreover, people express their emotions freely. This means they are not ashamed to admit they are not doing OK by themselves. So do not use expressions implying embarrassed sympathy or keeping a respectful distance, like "You will be all right," which may sound as though you do not care or are wishing the situation away (rather than showing that you have confidence in your friend's ability to deal with their problem). Real friends face everything together.

Criticism Is Care

An English-language teacher went to work in the interior of Brazil. On her birthday her students told her that she was an attractive woman, but that her clothes and haircut really didn't suit her. So, as a present, they took her shopping and picked out clothes for her. Then they escorted her to a hairdresser and instructed the stylist as to what to do.

Apprehensive, the teacher came to school the next day with her new makeover. On her way to work, people made comments about how nice she looked, which they had never really done before. She found that her "present" changed her from a demure, rather shy person to someone who was pleased with her appearance and grew in confidence as a result.

chapter five

BRAZILIANS AT HOME

WHO'S FAMILY?

For Brazilians family is an all-inclusive notion. "Close family" means parents, children, grandparents, uncles and aunts, cousins—everybody they see regularly for Sunday lunches and at family meetings (see Chapter 2). Moreover, relationships through marriage may be considered as strong as those through blood. In a case of marital breakup, it is not uncommon for the mother-in-law to take the side of her son- or daughter-in-law instead of her own child's.

Brazilians have the expression *ser parte da família* (to be part of the family), which refers to

anyone who is not related by blood or marriage but is considered as such. These may be close friends, godparents, or even a well-loved maid.

The connection between family employers and domestic employees is a complex one. Most middle-class Brazilians hire a part-time cleaner or a maid. While cleaners come on average once a week, maids work five to six days a week and many live with the family. The relationships can vary from downright abusive to turning-into-a-member-of-the-family, but they are rarely just professional. Some children become so attached to their maid (or nanny) that they maintain links with them throughout their adult lives. This is more common in regions where the influence from colonial times is strong, coupled with the fact that poverty is more widespread and the cost of labor is lower.

MARRIAGE

Weddings are an occasion to rejoice. Regardless of class or age group, a party is always the order of the day. Brazilians even celebrate when

they are not getting married officially: people who decide to live together as partners also stage an event for family and friends, and are given presents to help them in their new life. They even refer to themselves as "married" and to each other as "husband" or "wife." Common law spouses who are in a stable relationship (*união estável*) have the same legal rights as those officially married.

In 2011 homosexual couples gained the right to have their stable relationships recognized by law the same way as heterosexual couples. In 2013, the National Council of Justice (*Conselho Nacional de Justiça*) ruled that homosexual couples could have their stable relationship recognized as marriage if they wished to do so.

Most Brazilians live at home until they get married, regardless of age. Some carry on living with their parents after marriage, together with their new family. This situation is normally intended as provisional while they are working for the means to move somewhere else. Sometimes widowed parents or those on low incomes go to live with a son or daughter and their families.

MACHO MEN

Machismo is more noticeable toward the North and the interior of the country, where men have the last word, at least in public. In reality power usually rests with the breadwinner. Normally that is the man, though in major cities some women earn more than their partners. In that case, common decisions and responsibilities tend to be shared. Within the household, whatever the income earning ratio, a few areas remain quite

traditional: the woman will decide on the decor
and the man will choose the family car.

CHILDREN

The birth of a baby is the ultimate cause for
celebration. Babies are mostly born in hospitals.
Bigger city hospitals, especially after a caesarian
section, try to restrict the number of visitors in
the room at one time. Brazilians take turns and
try a *jeitinho* to get as many relatives and friends
in to see the newborn baby as soon as they can.

Children are the center of family life. Daily
routine is focused around them. Parents adapt
their mealtimes to suit the children's needs,
particularly when they are at school, since
children tend to eat most meals with their
parents. Grandparents play a fundamental role
in bringing up the offspring, especially in the
lower classes.

The way Brazilians take their children's
opinions and preferences into account may

astonish people from cultures where "children are seen but not heard." Their opinions will be listened to when deciding where to go on vacation. When shopping for clothes, children often decide what they like. When accompanying their parents to restaurants, children choose what they want to eat and drink. In fact, Brazilian restaurants are very child friendly. Often, once the child has finished eating, while the adults carry on talking, the child will get up and talk to people from other tables or play with other children. This does not upset anyone. On the contrary, it is well received.

Discipline does not seem to be the most important issue. The relationship between Brazilian parents and their children is based more on affection and the respect that comes out of it.

In the bigger cities, working parents tend to leave their young children in day care. There are public and private centers, with varying prices. Some of the best include nurses and psychologists on the staff and offer a busy program for entertaining and educating the children. Some workplaces also offer day-care facilities.

Middle- and upper-class schoolchildren can have very full schedules, attending extracurricular activities such as sports, music, dance, and language courses.

Families are larger in rural areas and smaller in the cities. A single child is increasingly becoming an option for the urban middle class, as they struggle to keep up with living expenses.

EDUCATION

Brazilians of all classes attach great importance to education. It is rightly seen as a passport to better employment and a higher standard of living.

The school year runs from February to the beginning of December. Schooling is divided into three sections: fundamental, intermediate, and higher. Basic education (fundamental) runs from seven to fourteen years old. This is free, as is intermediate (high school) education. Of course, there are private, fee-paying institutions that are often better resourced and provide better tuition than the state equivalents. University and further education is a mix of state funded and fee-paying, though the best universities in Brazil are free.

Education does not stop once you graduate. Professional Brazilians frequently enroll in courses outside office hours so as to keep up with an ever-changing work environment, stay one step ahead of the new graduate intake, and hold on to their jobs.

Although education is provided at all levels, the percentage of people who continue beyond basic education is low. Illiteracy is still a factor although rates have improved: in 2010 just over 9 percent were classified as illiterate. At the same time 5 percent of school-age children had never attended school. Not surprisingly illiteracy and nonattendance rates are higher in the poorer and more rural communities. Lack of education bars access to better employment, so people from these groups end up in menial jobs, which are so poorly paid that their children have to leave school earlier and start work as well. The government has been taking steps to combat this and provide incentives for school attendance through the *bolsa família* (see Chapter 1).

Military service is compulsory for men at age eighteen. It can vary from six months to one year.

EMPLOYMENT

Contrary to some of the stereotypes believed outside the country, in Brazil most people work very hard. There is no social welfare system, which means that once you have a job you work hard to keep it. Often people have more than one job to make ends meet. There is also a sizable black economy made up of people selling things on the street, washing car windows, reading palms, "looking after" parked cars, and so on. They live on the small change they receive and put many hours in just to get by. Those scratching out a living on the streets or on the land are probably not included in the official employment statistics.

What may seem surprising is that in the census taken in 2010 the age range for employment was from ten to seventy. Education is universally available, but in some poor households children have to work to help support the family. However, the number of children working has dropped to below 5 percent, with more working in rural areas than in the towns. People also retire earlier in the towns. The percentage of those in declared work across all age ranges in 2010 was 68–80 percent men and 56 percent women.

Most of the workforce is divided between three main sectors: the retail and service sector is the largest, followed by industry, and then the agricultural sector. Employment is higher in the South and Southeast and at its lowest in the Northeast. This explains why there has been so much migration from the Northeast to the South in search of work.

The minimum wage (*salário minimo*) is about US $300 a month. Normally house cleaners and other menial workers will receive this, but in major cities they may well earn more. Salaries vary according to profession and region.

HEALTH SERVICES

Although in theory all Brazilians should have free access to health services, the reality is very different. Everybody who can afford it pays for a private health plan and has regular medical checkups (the philosophy is one of prevention rather than waiting to fall ill and looking for a cure). In private health-care land, everything works. The patient can see any specialist he wants without going through a general practitioner first. Screenings, tests, and treatments are all available. For those who need to go to a hospital, some patient rooms look like hotel suites. On the other hand, apart from a few model hospitals, the public health system (*SUS: Sistema Único de Saúde*) has never-ending waiting lists. Nothing seems to function as it should and treatment often leaves much to be desired.

The middle ground seems to be covered by occupational health plans, provided by employers.

HOUSING

Walking down the street, you can see that Brazilians do not like their houses to be just like everyone else's, and certainly not like their neighbor's! Be it self-built or a sophisticated architectural design, individualism is the goal. The result can be an area with colonial-style buildings next to modern ones, next to others copied from distant lands. The city of Blumenau, in Santa Catarina, is built in a mock Bavarian style, because its German settler inhabitants felt like it.

In bigger centers, where space is at a premium
and the population more numerous, many people
live in apartment buildings. These are far more
anonymous and there is little one can do to
change the façade of one's home. But the lack
of individualism is compensated for by extra
security and the sharing of maintenance costs.
Some buildings house more people than a small
village and have internal gardens and playground
areas.

The other element that may attract an
outsider's attention is that Brazilians live behind
bars. In larger towns, windows and sometimes
doors are protected by iron bars to prevent them
from being broken into.

O sonho da casa própria (the dream of owning
your own home) is something everybody talks
about. Housing, however, is expensive,
particularly in the big cities. Many people rent.
In the Brazilian rental market the tenant provides
all the furniture and fixtures. Even though they

are able to decorate the place as they wish, most Brazilians long for a place they can call their own. As salaries are generally low and house prices high, for most the dream of owning a home remains just that.

SHOPPING

Many Brazilian towns have a day or two a week, one normally on the weekend, when some of their streets are taken over by open-air *feiras* (similar to farmers' markets) with fresh food stands. Besides fresh fruits and vegetables, you can normally buy fish, cheese, and even clothes or small plastic household items. Other places have specially dedicated buildings where the vendors take turns on different days of the week.

For all your other needs there is always the shopping mall. These have spread throughout the country. Hypermarket chains are also on the increase, offering food, clothes, furniture, domestic appliances, and electrical goods.

Small shops still exist, although they find it hard to compete with the bigger ones. Bakeries are among the small businesses that have a captive audience. In São Paulo, for example, it is not

uncommon for someone to breakfast in the
bakery around the corner before going to work.
There, people sit at a counter or at small tables,
like in a snack bar. A typical *paulista* breakfast
will include caffé latte (*pingado*), warm bread
with butter (*pão na chapa*), cheese bread (*pão
de queijo*), and a mixed fruit juice (*vitamina*),
preferably eaten while reading the morning news.

DAILY LIFE AND ROUTINE

Working-class days start early. In big cities, where
a cross-town journey can take a long time, some
people leave home in the early hours to line up
for already crowded buses. Office workers tend
to start working between 8:00 and 9:00 a.m.,
while most shops, particularly inside shopping
malls, do not open before 10:00 a.m.

A morning shower is the usual start to the day.
Breakfast varies depending on the region but

coffee with milk, bread with butter and/or cheese, and a piece of fruit are national staples.

Many people drive to work, especially the middle classes. City buses are notorious for being few and late. In cities served by underground trains, this is a better way to travel: clean, quick, and always on time. They can, however, be overcrowded in the rush hours. People tend not to eat on public transportation or on the street.

Lunch is taken between noon and 3:00 p.m., and can last from fifteen minutes up to two hours. In small towns people tend to return home for lunch. In bigger cities they usually eat out in restaurants. Some companies have their own eating facilities.

Working hours are flexible and some people work late. Dinners can be delayed as a result, but somewhere between 7:00 and 8:00 p.m. is normal.

Long working hours mean that families with children also stay up late. Parents like to play with their children when they get home. They normally watch the TV news and *novelas* together, and quite often everyone goes to bed about the same time.

Single people often spend their evenings attending evening courses, exercising at the gym, and going out, especially on Fridays.

chapter six

TIME OUT

Most Brazilians socialize outside the home. They
prefer to meet friends in shopping malls, squares,
bars, or restaurants, or to go to a movie with them.
And, of course, in the coastal towns there is the
attraction of the beach.

EATING OUT AND EATING IN

As a first option Brazilians from the cities will have
a meal with you in a restaurant rather than invite
you home. Young professionals eat out most
weekdays, and dinner can be late. A visitor should
not assume that they are escaping without paying

if someone says, "Would you like to come out for dinner?" Friends normally split the bill. If a man and a woman are having a meal, the man should offer to pay, although the offer may be declined.

There are fast-food outlets, of course, but a good option for many who are in a hurry and on a budget is the *comida por quilo* (food by the kilo). This is a self-service restaurant with a wide array of different dishes where you pay by quantity.

Beans or Pizza?

The most typical Brazilian food is beans and rice, though some people have joked that in fact it should be pizza. There is a popular saying that goes "In the end, everything finishes with pizza." (*No final, tudo acaba em pizza*). It refers to situations that are not properly resolved or where the solution to a problem is rushed and not thought through, just as when you go out with friends without planning anything beforehand and you end up having a pizza.

For a quick snack Brazilians may well go to a bar. It is unusual for people to just drink and they often eat *tira gostos*, snacks, rather like tapas.

A significant component of Brazilian cooking is meat-based, and nowhere is this more apparent than at a *churrascaria* (*rodízio*), a barbecue-style restaurant. For a fixed price you help yourself to salads and side dishes from a buffet and then sit and wait. Waiters appear with different types of meat on

spits, which they carve in front of you, and keep coming until you can eat no more.

Meat and buffet-style eating are also a feature of meals at people's houses. When Brazilians entertain at home, it is the custom to prepare many dishes, so that everyone can try a bit of whatever they want to. For those with balconies or yards there will always be a barbecue, and hosts and guests take turns in looking after the food. On more formal occasions, the best strategy is to wait for the host to indicate where the guests are to sit.

A QUICK COOK'S TOUR OF BRAZIL

Brazilian cuisine is regionally based and is quite varied. In the Northeast, you may well have *carne de sol*, also called *carne seca* (beef, salted and dried in the sun). In Bahia the food is cooked in palm oil and is often heavily spiced. There are also fish stews (*moqueca de peixe* or *vatapá*). In the South meat is again in evidence in the form of large barbecued steaks. Rio lays claim to *feijoada*, the national dish—a black bean stew with different cuts of pork, served with kale and a slice of orange.

For a "quick something," there are always *salgadinhos* (savory pastries), eaten with coffee, fruit juices, soft drinks, or beer in any *lanchonete* (snack bar). Brazilians do not snack on candy as much the British, but you can find *docinhos* (small homemade candies) in all *docerias* (cake and confectionery shops) and some snack bars.

DRINKING

When it comes to alcohol, Brazilians prefer beer, especially *estupidamente gelada* (ridiculously frozen). In bars and on beaches, beer bottles come in polystyrene or plastic containers to keep cool.

For something stronger there is *cachaça*—a spirit made from sugar cane. This forms the basis of *caipirinha* (add ice, crushed lime, and sugar). Much in the way that you find connoisseurs of whiskey, you discover lovers of *cachaça*, and there is a great variety of tastes and textures.

Wine is considered a more sophisticated option. It is drunk mainly toward the south where the climate is more conducive to its production. Most quality wines are imported, though Brazil is starting to produce good whites. Whatever the drink, it usually comes accompanied by food and is considered part of the overall enjoyment of an evening or occasion.

TIPPING

People normally round prices up, so do not expect small change back. Restaurants and bars usually include a service charge. If not, you should leave a 10 percent tip. You should also tip people who "look after your car" plus hotel and nightclub staff, when appropriate.

WHAT TO WEAR

Brazilians tend to believe that you are what you wear. When socializing in urban centers or doing business, dressing smart is the norm. In other situations clothes are color coordinated but informal—particularly when the weather is hot.

Dressing down can be used to the visitor's advantage, as a way to avoid unwanted attention, particularly in rough areas. Unfortunately, though, this may also stop you from being admitted to, or well treated at, the restaurant of your choice.

Very few places ask for formal wear, apart from a few nightclubs. In beach resorts that are also big cities, going to a restaurant in town in your beachwear may not be well received.

WHERE BRAZILIANS MEET UP
The Beach

In coastal towns the beach is the favorite meeting place for people of all ages, a focal point for getting together, flirting, walking, talking, and playing recreational sports. The elderly and families with young children prefer early mornings, while couples prefer late afternoons and evenings for that walk along the sand. Health campaigns advising on sun care are having an effect, even though

long-ingrained habits are difficult to break and Brazilians still sunbathe in the hottest hours of the day.

For those who want to escape the sun, there are bars and stands where you can eat fried fish and all sorts of seafood. To drink there are cold beer, *caipirinha*, or *água de côco* (coconut water), which comes straight from fresh green coconuts.

Town Squares and Shopping Malls

In the interior, the town square is the place to meet, especially on the weekend. People go there to chat, play games (such as cards or dominoes), flirt, or just read the newspaper. In the cities shopping malls are taking over from the old town squares, particularly for youngsters. Others might meet there for lunch before the movies, to have a chat over a light snack, or to go window-shopping.

Sunday in the Park

Sunday mornings seem to be the time when park lovers arrive with their bicycles, jogging gear, or picnic baskets. The biggest parks have snack bars and restaurants inside them, and sometimes even museums, with workshops open to the public. There are also free concerts from well-known— and lesser-known—musicians on weekends.

Waterfalls

Brazilians from towns in the interior also try to get out on weekends and often take food, and even a whole barbecue kit, to a waterfall or river. This is usually a day trip and will involve leaving the car

and carrying the gear quite a distance. It may look as though you are in the middle of nowhere, but after a good hour walking you often find that someone else has gotten there first and that their barbecue is in full swing.

Markets and Fairs

A favorite weekend or holiday pastime for many people is to go around open markets and craft fairs. This is as much to stop and talk to the vendors about their goods as it is to buy anything.

Vacations

Brazilians take their annual vacations in one block of twenty to thirty days. They often travel for the whole of this break. People with children normally go away during school vacations. The idea of a short break to relax does not feature—relaxation comes with time.

SPORTS AND EXERCISE

Physical exercise is considered very important. You will see people walking, jogging, and cycling on beaches or in parks in the early hours of the morning. Gyms are also popular.

Interestingly though, sports are not seen as a means of getting fit, but rather as relaxation. Especially on town beaches, space is given over to volleyball and football (and even foot volleyball).

In apartment buildings there may well be a swimming pool for the residents to share, as well as a space for children to play games. Cycling is becoming increasingly popular and on Sundays special cycle lanes are set up in major cities for the growing band of two-wheel devotees.

When it comes to spectator sports there is football (soccer). Matches are played on Sundays and most major cities have at least one stadium, which teams share. As much as the spectacle of the game itself, there is the extravaganza of the crowd—where sports and music combine, with all manner of drummers and small trumpet bands playing all around the ground during the game.

Formula One motor racing is the second-biggest spectator sport. Brazil is visited once in the season and many enthusiasts will set their watches to catch other grand prix races live on television from around the world.

CULTURAL LIFE
Nighttime

In most major cities there is plenty to do after dark. Brazilians often go out late, eat out, and take in a show or some live music. Most people love to dance and there are clubs for all types of music, from traditional rhythms such as samba and *forró*, to imports such as salsa. In São Paulo and Rio there is a growing club scene with DJs from home and abroad, playing a fusion of house and dance rhythms with homegrown Latin grooves.

Music
Brazil has an incredibly rich musical heritage. Latin

rhythms, particularly the bossa nova, are one of the mainstays of jazz and there is a rich vein of experimental music, not to mention classical and different folk traditions. Live music is popular and some city councils sponsor live events. Where the artist is well known, the audience does not just watch, they join in, and often you find yourself in the middle of a huge sing-along.

With classical composers such as Villa Lobos, Brazil's musical tradition is not confined to popular music or jazz. Even in a region as seemingly remote as the Amazon, opera lovers can delight in a mixture of exoticism and international recognition. The Teatro Amazonas, in Manaus, has an annual opera festival in around April/May.

Theater and Cinema
Most cities have both multiplexes, often in shopping malls, and art house cinemas, and they are well attended. Cinema is regarded as an art form, not just a form of entertainment, and at the moment Brazilian cinema is alive and thriving. Film directors like Fernando Meirelles (*City of God*, *The Constant Gardener*) and Walter Salles (*The Motorcycle Diaries*) have gained international acclaim. Theatergoing is popular among the middle classes.

Museums and Galleries

Despite not having the museum culture of Europe or the USA, Brazilian cities today have a variety of museums and art galleries displaying domestic and foreign exhibits. São Paulo is a destination for international touring exhibitions.

Brazil's own baroque sacred art is exceptional, as are its naive, modernist, and contemporary pieces. Brazilian regional popular art is colorful, varied, intriguing, and highly creative.

The Museu Imperial in Petrópolis, in Rio de Janeiro state, Museu Histórico Nacional in the city of Rio de Janeiro, and Museu do Ipiranga in São Paulo are essential stops for those interested in Brazilian history.

chapter seven

TRAVEL, HEALTH, & SAFETY

GENERAL INFORMATION

Visas and Other Entry Requirements

Visa restrictions change from time to time and updates need checking. Brazil has a policy of reciprocity, which means that if a country starts asking for special visas for Brazilians, Brazil will do the same for citizens from that country. In 2013 US and Australian citizens needed to obtain a visa for any purpose before entering. UK citizens did not and were given a ninety-day visa on arrival. Everyone has to complete an immigration form on arrival, and keep it with them to hand back on departure. Losing it may result in delays leaving the country and a possible fine.

Bureaucracy

Every country has its seemingly impenetrable bureaucracy and Brazil is no exception. Bureaucrats do not like to be hurried and are supremely conscious of their power. It does not pay to get frustrated, or demanding. Brazilians have their own *jeitinho* for dealing with this or any other situation that involves lining up and waiting. Often they will go to the front of the line and just ask for some information (*só uma informação*), and the official may well deal with them then and there.

Getting a Visa Extension

In São Paulo, some years ago, outside the subway near the Federal Police station was a row of shops with official-looking people typing forms. I was waved into one so that someone could charge me for filling out a form and direct me to the police station nearby. Inside the station, and after I had "asked for information," the police filled out more forms and sent me to the Banco do Brasil (to pay for my visa and come back with the receipt).

In the bank they took the form I had filled out and paid for in the strange little shop. A German, who was waiting in line for the same reason, approached the counter, to be told that he did not have the requisite bank payment form. Apparently, the bank did not issue such forms and neither did the police. When he asked where he could acquire one, he was directed to a shop across the street that sold umbrellas.

Documents

Carry a form of identification at all times: the police have the right to ask for papers. Rather than carry the original, it is a good idea to have authenticated photocopies. This reduces the risk of losing a passport or having original papers stolen.

Insurance

There is only one rule here, particularly with regard to health: be insured. Health services for those who are insured are excellent. Much less positive comments could be made about the treatment available for those who are not (see page 112, under Health Services).

Cars, however, are often not insured and people do not insure their belongings in the same way that they might in Europe or the USA. Rental cars normally come insured, but check what type of insurance it is, and especially any excess liability in case of accident or breakdown.

Changing Money

Money can be changed at airports, in hotel lobbies, and in banks. In a bank, be prepared to line up with everyone else and to wait a while. Dollars and other hard currencies are accepted. Brazilians are careful when it comes to going to the bank, and with reason. People do not display their money: they fold notes and tuck them away, often separating them into different pockets and wallets. In big cities everyone is conscious of the possibility of being mugged. They only ever leave banks, or shops, or anywhere, once any cash is safely put away. ATMs exist, both inside banks and on the street, though the latter look like mini fortresses. It is safer to use those inside the banks. Avoid using the street ATMs, especially at night.

GETTING AROUND
Car

In Brazil, the car is king. Why walk when it is hot and cars have air-conditioning?

Driving is often fast, and it helps to know the way, since not everywhere is clearly signposted. Traffic is chaotic, little respect is paid to lanes, and drivers switch at will and without warning. In major cities traffic jams are frequent and using the horn is a routine feature of driving. Depending on the time, and the day, it can take ages to cross town or to get to the beach. At night people do not always stop at red lights: they slow down and continue moving if nothing is coming. Parking on the street can mean allowing someone to "look after" the car—for a small fee.

People are used to driving long distances: a six-hour drive is not unusual to go somewhere for the weekend. There are still dirt roads in many parts of

the interior and the roads that are surfaced often have large potholes in them. There are stories (and photos) of some holes being big enough to swallow a whole car.

The Federal Police can impose on the spot fines if a car is not in good working order. Some visitors have reported situations involving having to pay their way out of a problem with the traffic police. This approach should be treated with extreme caution as offering money up front may be interpreted as a bribe.

A visitor contemplating driving in Brazil is advised to carry an international driver's license. The major national and international car rental companies are generally very good (see Insurance, above).

Taxi

Taxis are generally cheaper in Brazil than in many other countries—São Paulo being the exception—and a relatively safe way to get around cities. They are usually marked "Taxi" and have a red number plate. Radio taxis, booked in advance by phone, are the best option, particularly in the evening.

In some areas there are also vans and minibuses (*lotação*) that operate a system halfway between taxis and buses, taking people together who are going the same way. Although these are becoming regulated in some cities, many are still illegal and should be avoided.

Bus

In Town

Buses are very cheap, quite crowded at rush hour, and can be difficult for outsiders to use, since bus stops in towns do not have destinations on them. Buses drive more erratically than cars. Different buses have different entrances and procedures for paying, so it's best to have money ready and follow what everyone else does. People on buses are both helpful and mistrustful. If someone is standing with heavy bags, it is quite usual for someone sitting to offer to carry them on their lap. Passengers may sometimes talk, but usually they are unwilling to

Long Distance

In Brazil long distances are covered by bus or by plane. Buses are taken by those who cannot afford the plane, have lots of time, or are afraid of flying. But in a crowded *rodoviária* (intercity bus station) in a major city, it looks as though everyone travels by bus.

It is always best to book in advance and turn up on time—intercity buses are usually punctual. On these buses people are slightly more willing to have a conversation, though they tend to keep to themselves.

Trains

Although there is no national rail network as such, urban trains (metros) are a good way to move around cities like Sao Paulo, Rio de Janeiro, Brasilia, Belo Horizonte, Porto Alegre, and Recife. However, there are stretches of track that are mainly a tourist attraction for enthusiasts. The train that runs from Curitiba to Paranaguá, in Paraná—the Serra Verde Express—is a good example. Built in 1885, the line follows the Serra do Mar mountain range, in the middle of the Atlantic forest, and stops in several places of interest. There are quite a few *Maria-Fumaças* (steam trains) running in places such as Campinas (São Paulo), Tiradentes (Minas Gerais), and Bento Gonçalves (Rio Grande do Sul). The Madeira–Marmoré train route in Acre (Amazon), built in 1913, is worth the ride.

Plane
As in any large country, planes are used like buses, and increasingly so with the introduction of budget airlines. Flights are usually efficient and the staff tend to be very friendly. Plane travel is more relaxing and more secure than going by road.

People are much more willing to engage in conversation—sometimes for the entire duration of the flight.

HEALTH AND SAFETY
Mother Nature

Travelers not used to tropical countries may be surprised by the attitude of some Brazilians to the countryside around them. Mother Nature is something to be treated with caution, and Brazilians—especially those from the towns—do just that. Grass can contain poisonous snakes or spiders. People going for a walk in wild areas do not tread softly so as not to disturb the animals: they make lots of noise so that the animals know they are coming and get out of the way. That way both survive. For Brazilians, the idea of spending a few days getting dirty, bitten by insects, and with the possibility of coming face-to-face with some of the nastier of God's creatures is far from appealing.

Conversely, people who live in areas where there is a high incidence of dengue fever or malaria seem almost blasé about it. Malaria is thought of as something that is treatable and will pass. Dengue is seen as an inconvenience—much like a bad flu. However, visitors, who will not have the same resistance or antibodies, should take all reasonable precautions and seek medical advice before traveling.

Being Alert and Blending In

On London's Underground trains there is an announcement that says, "Please keep your belongings with you at all times." Nowhere is this more appropriate than in Brazil. In a country with one of the most unequal distributions of wealth in the world, the desperate resort to any means to make a living.

Most people have stories of either themselves or of someone close to them being mugged or sometimes worse. The media feeds this paranoia by presenting real crime stories in lurid detail.

It is important not to stand out too much as a foreigner. Banks, public transportation (except planes), and even the street are potentially risky places and all Brazilians take precautions. It is not wise to wear jewelry or expensive watches, or walk around with a map, a camera, or to talk on a cool-looking cell phone. It is important to carry some cash at all times, but folded and tucked away in different pockets. Some Brazilians have two wallets: if they are attacked, they give away one wallet and still have one left. The general rule is to let belongings go—trying to hang on to them could lead to far worse consequences.

In the street, Brazilians keep their wits about them. Some women will not walk in the streets by themselves after dark as that could attract attention. They notice who is around them at all times and move to avoid problems if they can. This may sound stressful, but as with anything it is a question of learning to adapt.

Perhaps it is this pressure that causes Brazilians, who are highly materialistic and consumerist, to have an ambivalent attitude to possessions. They almost expect their belongings to disappear. There is also the contrast between a people who are on the one hand incredibly friendly, warm, and hospitable, and on the other totally mistrustful of strangers—especially other Brazilians.

BUSINESS BRIEFING

In Brazil business practices differ by region as well as by the size and structure of different firms. São Paulo is more international and this can be seen in the management style of its companies. However, there are still quite a few family-owned businesses, which adopt an organizational style that is more hierarchical and patriarchal. Rio de Janeiro is at the same time more relaxed and traditional than São Paulo, something that might be explained by the beach culture combined with aristocratic traditions lingering from the time when it was

Brazil's capital. As a generalization, the further north you go, the more conservative and hierarchical the business mentality will be.

Most foreigners work for international companies in large metropolitan areas. Regardless of where they are they will follow global management style, slightly colored by local influences.

BUSINESS HOURS

The usual working day consists of eight hours plus one to two hours' break for lunch. In most companies people start work at 9:00 a.m., but some others may start at 8:00 or 10:00 a.m. and work until 6:00 or 7:00 p.m. However, in many firms, although people have a fixed starting time, they often work late. More senior members of staff tend to start working later in the morning and carry on working until later in the evening.

The best time for scheduling meetings or appointments is between 10:00 a.m. and noon or 3:00 to 5:00 p.m., except in São Paulo, where appointments can usually be arranged throughout the day (and may include business lunches).

STATUS AND HIERARCHY

In contrast to other cultures where self-made business people are particularly admired, in Brazilian society coming from a good family background is also considered important. Moreover, inherited wealth is seen as a considerable plus.  Respect comes with status, social class, family, and education. Self-made people try to enhance their status by dressing well, showing intellectual interests, and entertaining stylishly. The formula is valid for foreign visitors, too. Demonstrating an interest in Brazilian history, literature, and music can be useful. On a business trip, staying in a first-class hotel is a must.

The notion of hierarchy is part of Brazilian business culture. This can be observed when watching people talk, for example, since Brazilians are used to defining social status, age, and rank when addressing each other (see page 64). In a business situation, one should not address Brazilians by their first names only unless invited to do so. Some people introduce themselves with the title and name or surname they prefer to be called by. If in doubt, wait to see how others address the person in question. If that is not possible, it is better to be more formal and use the title *Senhor(a)* or *Doutor(a)* accompanied by the first name.

Vertical hierarchy is built into company structure and management style, with work-related problems being solved by superiors. Important decisions tend to be made by senior members of staff and then implemented by the rest. A team is normally bound together by a strong leader, chosen by seniority and experience. Giving orders is an important part of a team meeting. However, leaders are expected to take care of their subordinates and consider the view of key managers before making a decision.

WOMEN AT WORK

In the major cities the attitude to women in the workplace is far removed from that of the more conservative interior of Brazil. Whether it is caused by the economic need for women to work outside the home, or by a desire for change in social status, the fact is that Brazilian women are increasingly joining the workforce. Many have college degrees and even outnumber men in areas such as education, journalism, law, and medicine. They own small companies, and sometimes inherit their father's family businesses. They do well in politics, too.

Although, in terms of comparative salary, women are still discriminated against, and there are a few conservative people who prefer to negotiate with men, foreign women should not have any problem in the Brazilian business scene.

DRESS CODE

Brazilians are fashion conscious and follow European styles. There are several current trends in business attire. Suits are normally tailor-made to have a perfect fit. Women dress "sexy" and elegant on all occasions.

The idea that "you are what you wear" applies to business culture with the addition of a new dimension. In Brazil there is a belief that the care someone takes with their appearance reveals the way they will care about their business.

Foreign male visitors should stick to good quality dark suits, long-sleeved shirts, conservative ties, polished, stylish shoes, and a good leather belt. Women should wear feminine dresses and suits or pantsuits plus impeccable shoes or sandals with medium "city" heels. Avoid blouses with bows and frills or big patterns. Single colors are best.

Special attention should be paid to details. Nails should be clean and manicured. Teeth should be kept immaculate. Women should not overdo their cosmetics. Brazilians wear very light make-up, with a tendency toward a more natural look, but often with a bright colored lipstick.

Depending on the destination and the time of year, light materials and natural fibers are most suited to the hot weather. Good, lightweight wool is preferable in São Paulo and in the South during winter. In the North and Northeast, where it is hot year-round, and depending on the industry, some men wear suit trousers and rolled up long-sleeved shirts. Be aware, though, that the temperature inside offices can be surprisingly chilly because of the air-conditioning. Also, even when Brazilians dress casually at their offices, they will expect visitors to wear proper business attire. Three-piece suits are fashionable in winter but look out of place in summer. Short-sleeved shirts with ties are considered ridiculous. So is wearing the colors of the Brazilian flag, yellow and green, together.

For business entertaining, dark suits are adequate formal wear. On more informal occasions, smart jeans with a nice shirt and a blazer can be acceptable. For women, a "little black dress" is always perfect.

Brazilian businesspeople wear stylish casual clothes even in their free time. So, a business visitor should make sure to dress well when shopping or going for a walk and resist the temptation to wear old sneakers and jeans.

MAKING CONTACT

The way Brazilians do business is through personal connections. They like to deal with people they know, either directly or to whom they have been introduced by someone they respect. If possible, an introduction from a mutual acquaintance is just the ticket for a successful start. It is possible to hire Brazilian consultants and contacts in specific industries who can help foreigners find their way through the paperwork and make the right connections.

In any case, appointments should be made at least two weeks in advance, and confirmed two days before. "Dropping in" on business or government offices without an appointment is totally unacceptable. Business trips and appointments should be scheduled away from holidays and festivals, particularly *Carnaval*. Meetings might be lengthy and the traffic between offices can take a good bite out of one's time. It is therefore sensible to allow two to three hours for each meeting and not to schedule more than two or three appointments a day. But expect them to be cancelled or rescheduled at short notice.

It is very rare for important deals to be done over the phone or by mail.

MEETINGS

In some regions people are casual about punctuality. This is not the case in parts of Rio and São Paulo, where meetings normally start on time. Either way, when scheduling and arriving for a meeting, it is wise to be prepared for some degree of tardiness and not to show annoyance with it. Furthermore, while senior executives and managers may arrive late, foreign visitors are always expected to arrive on time.

In most offices, a *cafezinho* (literally, "little coffee") will be offered upon arrival. It is usually dark and strong and served in espresso cups. This is a traditional way of showing hospitality. Coffee and water are served several times during the day.

While the British start with small talk and North Americans go straight to the point, Brazilians do a little socializing beforehand. It tends to happen around the drinking of *cafezinho* (as you arrive and before you leave) and is a mixture of small talk and a little investigation, when the visitor can be casually asked about their background, interests, mutual acquaintances, or anything that will help the Brazilian businessperson get a feel for whom they are dealing with. The amount of social chat varies from region to region and the best practice is just to wait for the Brazilian to indicate they are ready to get down to business.

An exception may be São Paulo, where the "time is money" mentality applies. There, introductory conversation tends to last just a few minutes before business starts in earnest. But do not think that establishing a personal relationship is not important to *paulistas*. This will take place during business lunches and entertaining, once they know they are interested in the deal.

In the meeting the seating plan is normally hierarchical. In companies used to interacting with foreigners the meeting might be conducted in English. In this case, foreign visitors should remember to speak more slowly and use shorter sentences, making sure they are being perfectly understood. In some situations, an interpreter may also be present. In this case, remember to direct the conversation and look at the Brazilian businessperson instead of the interpreter. In any case, learning a few words and expressions in Portuguese will help break the ice and show you are making an effort. For meetings conducted in Portuguese, you will find that Brazilians are fast talkers, so you may need to ask them to slow down a little. (Do not volunteer to speak Spanish unless asked to do so.)

Brazilians look straight into the eyes of the person they are talking to. Although that may feel intrusive to some visitors, it is important not to shy away, lest you give the impression of having something to hide.

It is normal for a meeting to be quite lively, with a few interruptions. Don't be surprised if conversations appear to stray from the topic. Brazilians tend to multitask more than people in the US and UK. One thing prompts another and focus is maintained within a bigger picture. Also, if someone interrupts the meeting to answer the phone, that does not mean they are not interested in the business at hand.

During conversations, visitors should not be alarmed at being interrupted in the middle of a sentence. Brazilians tend to overlap their points of view. In fact, the more interested they are in a subject, the louder and more overlapping the discussion will be. Some of the interjections may also sound confrontational, but, again, it is only their way of reacting (and paying attention) to the conversation. Brazilians tend to avoid direct confrontation and prefer a more indirect way of demonstrating disagreement.

Brazilians like to analyze situations thoroughly and do not rush meetings until they are ready to be concluded, regardless of time schedules.

Exchanging business cards—printed in both English and Portuguese—is part of the protocol when being introduced or on leaving. Outsiders should resist the temptation to rush away once the meeting is over. Taking your time to greet and say good-bye is part of the effort of building a relationship and typical of the business culture.

PRESENTATION STYLE

Brazilians tend to consider the personality and attitudes of their counterparts in order to decide if they want to deal with them in business. Charts, favorable data, and good organizational skills are fundamental, but alone they will not do the trick. Brazilians are happy to talk and hear about personal achievements and show their human side. Confidence, eloquence, and an ability to explain oneself are important, too.

Presentations should be expressive. More attention is paid to content, but style counts a great deal. They should also be kept short (around thirty minutes), use visual materials, and be followed by discussion and debate. Brazilians are interested in new ideas provided that they are supported by facts and research. They can talk at length—and at high volume—using expressive body language. In return, they expect people to explain themselves fully.

WORK AND PLAY

When I arrived at work one morning, in an NGO in Olinda, Pernambuco, I was informed that the annual report needed to renew financial support from a multinational company was due on the following day. The writing hadn't really begun, so everybody was asked to spend the day in a meeting to produce the document.

Halfway through the day we heard animated sounds coming from outside. One by one my colleagues went to the window, noticed a *troça* (small group of people playing and rehearsing for *Carnaval*) going down the hill and left the meeting to follow the dance! In a minute I was the only one left. Uncertain of what to do, and panicking a little, I continued working.

They all returned half an hour later, full of energy. They worked frantically through the night, produced a first-class report, and the multinational renewed its support.

During presentations, persuasion, politeness, respect, courtesy, and boldness are qualities that Brazilian businesspeople look for.

NEGOTIATIONS

Changing a negotiating team can ruin a perfectly good deal in Brazil, since the trust is placed as much in the negotiators as in the company they represent. Also, it is considered bad business practice that goes against Brazilian protocol.

When doing business in Brazil, be aware that it may take a few trips to negotiate an agreement. One should not show disappointment if a signed contract is not achieved at the first meeting.

Brazilians are quite analytical and tend to look at each different situation individually. They prefer to let negotiations develop at a relatively slow pace, leaving details to be considered later in the game. Some hype is expected at the beginning, in the knowledge that not all the initial information will be totally accurate. They will argue their case passionately and enjoy the debate, always looking for constructive solutions rather than confrontation or an outright "no."

Brazilians solve their disagreements face-to-face, through conversation, without putting things in writing and very rarely going to a third party. Agreements and concessions will be made slowly, through successive meetings. Even when decisions are reached quickly, they may be modified in detail before being implemented.

It is crucial, therefore, not to impose tight deadlines when negotiating.

CONTRACTS

When doing business in Brazil, foreigners should find local accountants and lawyers to work with on contractual issues. Using nonlocal professionals may be interpreted as mistrust and cause offense. Also, if there seems to be a problem that is impossible to solve, Brazilian accountants and lawyers will usually find a way around it (*jeitinho*).

It is part of the Brazilian protocol that documents are not normally signed immediately after the parties reach an agreement, but are prepared to be signed later. A written agreement, however, may still not be binding. It may change from the version that was agreed upon, and may change again subsequently. In Brazil, in contrast to cultures that view the contract as the last word, a contract can be revisited and modified as work progresses, and deadlines can change.

GIFTS

During the initial meetings it is not necessary to bring a gift. It is better to offer to buy lunch—or even dinner—while trying to find out their taste. A social occasion may be the best opportunity for gift giving. It is important, though, not to choose anything that is apparently expensive and can be mistaken for a bribe, or which may cause embarrassment.

Inexpensive cameras, nice pens, and small electronic items, such as calculators, address books, or personal CD players, are good choices.

Avoid practical or personal presents (such as perfume or sunglasses) and anything in the colors black and purple (associated with mourning).

If invited to a Brazilian's home, consider it a special honor and indication of friendship. Bring some wine, champagne, whiskey, or chocolate, together with a small house present plus something for the children (see page 100, under Invitations Home). Send flowers with a thank-you card on the following day.

BUSINESS ENTERTAINING

In Brazil, time spent socializing goes toward constructing successful business relationships. People say things like "for friends, everything; for enemies, the law," which goes some way to showing that, in business, Brazilians value relationships over formal agreements.

Restaurant entertainment, rather than at home, is the norm. Breakfast meetings are rare. Lunch and dinner meetings are part of the routine. Punctuality is expected at business meals or meetings at restaurants. Shaking hands with everyone present is the usual greeting upon arrival and departure.

Meals can be quite lengthy: at least two hours for lunch and about three for dinner. Lunch is normally scheduled between noon and 2:00 p.m. Dinner can start anytime after 7:00 p.m., while dinner parties can take place around 10:00 p.m. and often go on into the early hours.

A business meal is an opportunity for both parties to get acquainted and comfortable with each other. It is all about developing the relationship. Brazilians may ask questions that sound too personal or intrusive. You can politely avoid the question, or give an evasive answer.

Business itself is not usually discussed during meals. Visitors should wait for their Brazilian companions to raise business issues, which tends to happen during coffee toward the end of the meal.

Brazilians always wash their hands before eating and rarely touch food with their fingers, using paper napkins to get hold of any bread or *salgadinhos* (savory pastries) that may be served as a starter. They use their knife, not their fork, to cut everything, including fruit. A napkin is used in between eating and drinking; using a toothpick in public is considered bad manners (but acceptable when covering the mouth with your other hand). If toasted by your companions, you should always return the compliment with another toast.

If entertaining a business associate, choose a prestigious restaurant, if possible with a cuisine typical of your country. If in doubt, ask their secretary to recommend a place. When hosting a meal, make sure that the most important seat is reserved for the highest-ranking guest. Waiters do not usually bring checks until they are asked for and tipping is normally 10 percent.

If you decide to invite Brazilians to dinner or a party at home, do not ask them to bring food or drink, or expect them to be on time. And never suggest a time for the party to finish.

KEEPING IN TOUCH

A foreign businessperson should not expect to do much business on a first visit, but should allocate enough time and money to establish a long-term business relationship. Coming back regularly is part of the package, since many Brazilian executives dislike sporadic short visits by foreign sales representatives.

Brazilians build relationships mainly through face-to-face contact. Phone calls are the second-best option for keeping in touch. "Cold" letters and e-mails may not get an answer.

When phoning a Brazilian contact, it is important to spend a little time on social conversation before launching into business, and not to cut the call short once the subject is sorted out.

USEFUL BUSINESS HINTS

- The office secretary is the person to consult regarding any questions you may have. Treat her nicely and she will help you through.
- Slow pace and informality are characteristics of Brazilian business culture (with the exception of São Paulo), but there may be a formal atmosphere during the first meetings.
- Knock on office doors: then stand and wait.
- When lost for a topic of conversation, traveling, food, arts, sports, and football can be useful. Avoid talking about personal matters, ethnicity, the economy, and Argentina (particularly Argentina's football team). Use the word football, not soccer.
- Brazilians are not Hispanics and do not like being addressed in Spanish. Nor should you use the word Latins to refer to them.
- Brazilians are Americans (from South America) and have an aversion to the term America being used to designate the USA.
- Note, when looking at figures, that in Brazil periods (full stops) are used to designate thousands and commas to indicate fractions.

chapter nine

COMMUNICATING

LANGUAGE

In Brazil, people speak Portuguese and not a lot
else. In tourist offices and in business you may find
some who speak a bit of English, but generally very
few people do and certainly not in restaurants,
shops, or other places where a visitor might interact
with the locals. Neither do Brazilians really

speak Spanish, although a number think
they do. Learning to speak Portuguese is
useful, both from a communication and
a security point of view. It is important,
especially in major cities, not to draw
attention to yourself. Speaking English in
a loud voice will certainly not help.

BODY LANGUAGE

Brazilians have a relaxed body language. They are a
tactile people, and putting a hand on someone when
talking to them is simply an indication of interest
in the conversation, nothing more. A handshake
between men may well be accompanied by the
other hand being placed on the shoulder.

In terms of body distance, people can be in close
proximity to each other and not feel that their

private space is being invaded. On the contrary, backing away can be considered rude. Brazilians also maintain eye contact when listening or talking to someone. They accompany their conversation with a whole series of gestures. Across cultures, the same gesture may have different meanings and the one to avoid in Brazil is the thumb-to-index-finger ring sign that means "good" in Anglo-Saxon societies. In Brazil it has a rather rude meaning that can get you into trouble. It is also considered bad manners to yawn or stretch in public.

HELLOS AND GOOD-BYES

Introductions can be quite formal. Men will shake hands and women will kiss on the cheek—twice if they are single, three times if they are married, but just once in São Paulo—as will men to women. In groups, people will often introduce themselves to each member in this way. The same ritual is repeated when leaving and is accompanied by quite long statements about how much the meeting was enjoyed, how it was good to see you, and how you should take care, as well as passing on best wishes to family (or friends and partners) who were unable to be there. In the middle of good-byes, someone can remember to say something and restart a conversation. In this case, once the topic is finished, the farewell proceedings will start again from the beginning. This good-bye ritual is often maintained in phone conversations as well. Even among close friends, the host tends to accompany the guest to the door. Announcing you are leaving and simply walking to the door without waiting for your host to accompany you can be considered rude.

CONVERSATION STYLE

Conversation, especially in groups, is lively, dynamic, and often noisy. Normally everybody seems to be talking at once. Interruption is frequent—often people do not get to finish what they are saying before someone else jumps in. However, no one is offended by this. Conversations may become wide-ranging and stray across many different points before returning to the original one.

Brazilians have a flirty way of talking, which particularly applies to communication between genders. They normally compliment each other about their looks, hairstyle, or choice of clothes. Sometimes they even imply something more sexual, or suggest going out together, without really meaning it. Unfortunately, the only difference between a real flirtatious conversation and a pretend one seems to be in the latter's slightly more jokey tone of voice.

HUMOR

Brazilians have a vivid and often quite black sense of humor, which is not always politically correct. They will make jokes about most things, including themselves, and there is a thriving wave of satire aimed at whichever politician is in power. Making fun of religion, though, can be a delicate issue and is be avoided.

Less well-educated people sometimes have a simpler sense of humor: the differences can be seen in TV comedies, which vary enormously from slapstick to more sophisticated lampooning of political leaders and social institutions.

THE MEDIA

Most of Brazilians' information comes from the TV. Nearly everyone, regardless of social status or remoteness, has a set. The major TV channel is Globo, one of the largest TV networks in the world, followed by SBT, Record, and Bandeirantes, among other national broadcasters. The majority of the television industry is privately owned, though there are public networks (TV Cultura and TV Brasil) that aim to provide both entertainment and education. The most

popular shows are *novelas*, news, and sports programs. Paid cable and satellite channels are the option of choice for the middle classes, while new Internet channels have a growing number of followers among the young.

Foreign language films or shows on TV are normally dubbed into Portuguese, but stereo TV sets come with PSA or SAP (Secondary Audio

Program) keys, which enable the viewer to watch most films with the original soundtrack.

There is a vast array of radio stations. Generally they are divided according to musical genre and there are also information and discussion channels. The musical stations (FM) do not generally have DJs who talk over songs. On the other hand, on talk radio (AM), the personality of the radio presenter is all that matters. There is also a multitude of online radios catering to all tastes.

As Brazil is so large, newspapers are generally regional, though some have a national reputation and a wider circulation. Most prominent are *Folha de São Paulo* and *Jornal do Brasil*, followed by *O Estado de São Paulo* and *O Globo*. The best-known national weekly magazines are *Istoé*, *Veja*, and *Época*.

All the main newspapers are also available on-line. Both *Folha de São Paulo* (www1.folha.uol.com.br/internacional/en) and the business newspaper *Valor Econômico* (www.valor.com.br/international) have online English versions.

Brazil has around 100 million Internet users. In 2012, it led the world in Facebook growth with 30 million people joining the site. Brazilians are also among the most engaged with social media, which is becoming as much part of their routine as watching TV. In 2012, it was reported that 43 percent of Brazilians watched TV while on social media, with 29 percent commenting about what they were watching.

POSTAL AND ELECTRONIC COMMUNICATION

Postal Service

There is a marked difference in the quality of service between registered and unregistered mail. Many Brazilians do not trust the unregistered mail of the *correio* (postal service). Important letters or parcels are sent by registered post, for which there are several options depending on urgency and weight. These are all more expensive than the ordinary delivery but they are very good. This also applies to mail going to or coming from abroad.

For domestic mail, the best service for documents or parcels is SEDEX. For international deliveries, there are other options: Sedex Mundi for any destination abroad, Sur Postal for countries belonging to the South American economic group Mercosul, and EMS for all other countries. EMS has a range of services and delivers in two to five working days depending on the country and the service. For more information on these and other on-line services, go to www.correios.com.br.

Telephone

Public telephones (*orelhões*) can be easily found, even though they may not always be in working order. To use an *orelhão* (literally, "big ear"), you need to have a telephone card— bought in most *mercadinhos* (grocers), *papelarias* (stationers), and at street stands. However, *celulares* (cell phones) are widely used and have largely replaced the need for

public phones. Not all cell phones work in Brazil because of the difference in frequencies. If your home cell phone does work here, it may be a good idea to buy a local SIM card with prepaid minutes.

There are a few different operators to choose from when making interstate (DDD—*Discagem Direta à Distância*) or international calls (DDI— *Discagem Direta Internacional*); their numbers and prices vary from state to state, but you can always use Embratel, which is the national company and has the same number (21) anywhere in the country. So, if you want to call overseas, you need to dial the international access code (00), then the operator code (21 for Embratel), the country code, the area code (minus the initial 0), and the phone number.

Thus, to call the London number 020 7234 5678, you would dial 00 21 44 20 7234 5678. To call the USA you would need to dial 00, then the operator code, then 1 for the USA, followed by the seven-digit phone number.

When calling Brazil from abroad, dial your country's international access code (00 from the UK), then Brazil's country code (55), the code for the area (for example, 11 for São Paulo), and finally the eight-digit phone number. So, for São Paulo 1234 5678, from the UK, you should dial 00 55 11 1234 5678. From the USA you would need to dial 011 55 and then the area code and the number.

USEFUL TELEPHONE NUMBERS

Police 190

Federal Highway Patrol 191

Ambulance 192

Fire Brigade 193

International call via operator 0800 70 32 111

National call via operator 0800 70 32 110

National and international collect calls 0800 703 21 21

Rio de Janeiro and São Paulo also have numbers for special Tourist Police:

Rio de Janeiro (021) 3399 7170 (24 hours)

São Paulo (011) 3214 0209 (011) 3107 5642

COMPUTERS

In major cities many cafés have wi-fi. Hotels normally have facilities for Internet users. For plugging in your own laptop, you will need an AC adapter and a plug adapter. Some areas of Brazil are on 110 volts, while others are 220 volts, so you should check before you plug in. Also, electricity is not always constant in Brazil, and to cope with peaks and falls in current, most Brazilians have a voltage stabilizer connected between the electricity mains and their computer.

CONCLUSION

Having reached the end of this book, you will, we hope, have found a starting point from which to explore the different Brazils. If it all seems too much to take in, don't worry. Few Brazilians have been to more than three regions, if that. This is a country to experience bit by bit, contradiction by contradiction, and hopefully to begin to blend into and become part of. This will not be hard, since Brazilians are so welcoming. But because they are so welcoming and easy to befriend, leaving can be unsettling. On the other hand, what better opportunity to finally understand the meaning of the word *saudade*?

Further Reading

Bailey, S and M. Peria. *Racial Quotas and the Culture War in Brazilian Academia*. Sociology Compass (Vol. 4.8), Wiley Online Library, 2010.

Barrientos, A. *The Rise of Social Assistance in Brazil*. Development and Change (Vol. 44. 4), Wiley Online Library, 2013.

Bellos, Alex and Socrates. *Futebol, A Brazilian Way of Life*. London: Bloomsbury, 2009.

Brainard, Lael and Leonardo Martinez-Diaz (eds.). *Brazil As an Economic Superpower? Understanding Brazil's Changing Role in the Global Economy*. Washington: Brookings Institution Press, 2010.

Davidson, James Dale. *Brazil is the New America*. New Jersey: Wiley & Sons, 2012.

Fausto, Boris and Arthur Brakel. Cambridge: Cambridge University Press, 1999.

Hervieu, Benoit and Luis Gustavo Pacete, and Pâmela Pinto. *Brazil, The Country of Thirty Berlusconis*. Reporters Without Borders, http://en.rsf.org/brazil, 2013.

Insight Guides: Brazil. (7th ed.) London: Insight Guides, 2012.

Oliveira, Jaqueline. *Brazil—A Guide For Businesspeople*. New York: Intercultural Press, 2001.

Page, Joseph. *The Brazilians*. Cambridge, Massachusetts/New York: Da Capo, 1996.

Palin, Michael. *Brazil*. London: Weidenfeld & Nicolson, 2012.

Ribeiro, Darcy. *The Brazilian People: The Formation and Meaning of Brazil*. Gainesville, Florida: University of Florida, Center for Latin American Studies, 2000.

Riordan, Roett. *The New Brazil*. Washington: Brookings Institution Press, 2010.

Robinson, Alex. *Brazil Footprint Handbook*. Bath: Footprint Travel Guides, 2011

Rohte, Larry. *Brazil on the Rise: The Story of a Country Transformed*. New York: Palgrave MacMillan, 2012.

Rottgen, Raphael. *The Brazilian Dream: How I left my Finance Job in London and became an Entrepreneur in Brazil*. Charleston: Createspace, 2012.

Skidmore, Thomas E. *Brazil, Five Centuries of Change* (2nd ed). New York/Oxford: Oxford University Press, 2009.

Useful Web Sites

GOVERNMENT SITES
www.brasil.gov.br
www.ibge.gov.br
www.mre.gov.br
www.brazil.org.uk
www.washington.itamaraty.gov.br

BUSINESS SITES
www.executiveplanet.com
www.brazilbiz.com.br
www.brazil.doingbusinessguide.co.uk
www.doingbusiness.org
www.export.gov/brazil

GENERAL INFORMATION
www.brazil-factoid.com
www.brazzil.com
www.caranval.com
www.gringoes.com.br
www.terramistica.com.br
www.maria-brazil.org
www.globo.com.br
www.bbc.co.uk/brazil

culture smart! brazil

Index

Acknowledgments

With special thanks to Miguel Barbosa and Fernando Branco for their patience and assistance with the research, Cláudio Margolis for his thoughtful feedback, Romero Brito and João Carlos Araújo for their expert insights, and Heródoto Barbeiro, for finding time in his busy schedule.